THE FORAGER'S HANDBOOK

A Seasonal Guide to Harvesting Wild, Edible & Medicinal Plants

VICKIE SHUFER
author of *The Everything Guide to Foraging*

Skyhorse Publishing

Copyright © 2022 by Vickie Shufer
Illustrations copyright © 2022 by Vickie Shufer

All rights reserved. No part of this book may be reproduced in any manner without the express written consent of the publisher, except in the case of brief excerpts in critical reviews or articles. All inquiries should be addressed to Skyhorse Publishing, 307 West 36th Street, 11th Floor, New York, NY 10018.

Skyhorse Publishing books may be purchased in bulk at special discounts for sales promotion, corporate gifts, fund-raising, or educational purposes. Special editions can also be created to specifications. For details, contact the Special Sales Department, Skyhorse Publishing, 307 West 36th Street, 11th Floor, New York, NY 10018 or info@skyhorsepublishing.com.

Skyhorse® and Skyhorse Publishing® are registered trademarks of Skyhorse Publishing, Inc.®, a Delaware corporation.

Visit our website at www.skyhorsepublishing.com.

10 9 8 7 6 5 4 3

Library of Congress Cataloging-in-Publication Data is available on file.

Cover design by David Ter-Avanesyan
Cover photos by Evan Rhodes

Print ISBN: 978-1-5107-6786-7
Ebook ISBN: 978-1-5107-6787-4

Printed in the United States of America

Dedicated to Jim Duke, who introduced me to the world of medicinal plants and changed my life forever.

TABLE OF CONTENTS

Introduction   vii

Part 1: Foraging as a Lifestyle   1
Chapter One: Connecting with Nature   3
Chapter Two: Sustainable Foraging   7
Chapter Three: Benefits of Foraging   11
Chapter Four: Botany Basics   13

Part 2: Follow the Seasons (Plant Cycles)   19
Chapter Five: Spring   21
Chapter Six: Summer   27
Chapter Seven: Autumn   33
Chapter Eight: Winter   37

Part 3: Food "Farm"acy   43
Chapter Nine: Kitchen Lab   45
Chapter Ten: Wild Herbal Seasonings and Spices   51
Chapter Eleven: Herbal Teas   55
Chapter Twelve: Herbal Vinegars and Syrups   61
Chapter Thirteen: Tinctures, Cordials, and Elixirs   65
Chapter Fourteen: Herb-Infused Oils   69

Part 4: Meet the Herbs   71

Nutritional Glossary   157
List of Recipes   160
Index   161
Acknowledgments   166
About the Author   167

INTRODUCTION

"Foraging behavior is a trait of the human species."
—*The Origins of Human Diet and Medicine*

Have you ever wondered what it would be like to live a lifestyle of gathering wild plants growing around you and using them on a daily basis as your food and medicine? Or to go to the fields or swamps to gather a particular herb to treat a common ailment rather than a drugstore? *The Forager's Handbook* serves as a guide for living this lifestyle and provides the link between people and plants. Learn what plants to gather, when to harvest, what plants can be used for, and how to prepare them.

Foraging has been a part of my life for as long as I can remember. As a young child growing up on a farm in rural Kentucky, we gathered wild berries in the summer and harvested nuts in the fall. Winter was spent sitting around the wood stove cracking and shelling nuts. I was initially intrigued by the wild flavors but more importantly that you could go to the woods or fields to find a snack to eat without having to go to the store.

In my college years I took a number of botany classes, including one on poisonous and edible plants. I soon realized that there were far more wild edible plants and flavors than I had previously known, and I began experimenting in the kitchen to develop my own recipes.

For years people asked me if I also made medicine. I always responded that I would rather eat than be sick until I heard Dr. James Duke's

presentation on medicinal herbs at a wildflower symposium in the early 1990s. It was then that I realized food can be medicine and medicine can be food. You don't have to wait to get sick to use herbs. Using wild herbs as a part of your daily diet can enhance wellness and prevent illness before it happens.

Meeting Dr. James Duke changed my perspective on plants. I became a follower of Duke and attended many of his classes and workshops. Eventually I went back to school at Maryland University of Integrative Health and got my master's degree in therapeutic herbalism.

This book is a culmination of all that I've learned and shows you how to live the way of the forager throughout the year. In the spring are the greens, providing us with essential vitamins and nutrients. At the hottest, driest time of the year, we get sweet, juicy fruits to hydrate and strengthen us. In the fall are starchy roots and nuts that can be dried and stored for the winter to provide fat and protein. We get what we need when we need it and there is always something available. When the earth provides, the benefits are many.

References

Johns, T. (1996). *The origins of human diet and medicine*. Tucson, AZ: The University of Arizona Press.

PART 1

FORAGING AS A LIFESTYLE

Living the life of a forager is to live a life connected to plants and spending a lot of time outdoors. A forager follows the cycles and knows when the first plants emerge in the spring, when they bloom and produce fruit, and when they die back and go to seed.

A forager also spends a lot of time in the kitchen cleaning, processing, and preparing the harvest for food and medicine. This is where the magic happens. It is a form of alchemy, transforming plain and simple ingredients into a wonderful gourmet dish or a magical remedy for some ailment. The kitchen is like a chemistry lab where you mix and blend chemicals (in this case, phytochemicals) to get a final product.

Wild plants are a part of a forager's daily diet. When an ailment presents itself, a forager goes to the herbal apothecary to get the remedy. Using herbs in your daily diet is a way of preventing illness. Don't wait until you get sick to use herbs.

CHAPTER ONE

CONNECTING WITH NATURE

People-Plant Relationships   4

Forest Bathing   4

Mindfulness   5

Use the Senses (Organoleptics)   5

Journaling   5

References   6

People-Plant Relationships

Dr. James Duke once told me that our genes evolve with the plants growing around us, and those are the plants we should eat. In other words, plants have developed mechanisms for dealing with environmental stresses over time, such as secondary metabolites, phytochemicals that protect the plant and may be expressed in the color, shape, smell, or taste of the plant. Many of these secondary metabolites are medicine for people, who have to deal with the same environmental stresses as the plants. The plants growing around us, and especially the wild plants, are our medicine and what we should be eating.

HOMEOSTASIS

Homeostasis is a case of mind-body interaction that enables the body to heal itself through the use of needed phytochemicals to bring the body back into healthy balance. Our bodies are able to pick and choose those phytochemicals that are needed and discard the rest through the process of elimination (Duke, 2007).

Herbs and wild food are a mix of thousands of phytochemicals that have biological activities that have coevolved with our bodies for thousands of years. Our body has evolved with the wild diet that our ancestors consumed rather than the processed diet and synthetic pharmaceuticals that have been with us for less than two hundred years. Your ancestors' genes are the ones that your body recognizes, so your diet should include plants from your ancestors' countries of origin. Many of these phytochemicals are medicinal and essential for life. The herbs have a menu of phytochemicals that your body recognizes and is able to use them when they are needed, eliminating those it does not need (Duke, 2007).

WILD VERSUS TAME

The wild plant is better medicine than the agriculturally tamed plant. Many of our maladies are a result of not getting the phytochemicals that our bodies need to be healthy. Wild, untended ancestors of food plants produce more secondary metabolites, often medicinal, than cultivated plants (Duke, 2007).

Not only are wild plants better medicine but they are also easier to grow. Cultivated members of the mustard family are subject to infestation of the white cabbage butterfly unless some form of pesticide is used. Wild mustards don't have that problem. The same is true with wild beans. No bean beetles on the wild ones. The plant's defenses have been bred out of many of the cultivated vegetables.

Metabolites

Substances derived from plants are primary and secondary metabolites and are common to all plants.

- **Primary metabolites** contribute to the growth and development of the plant and include chlorophyll, amino acids, proteins, simple sugars, carbohydrates, vitamins, minerals, and plant hormones. The amounts vary but most are common to all plants.
- **Secondary metabolites** play a defensive role against herbivores and pathogens.

Forest Bathing

One way to connect with the natural world is through a form of mindfulness referred to as forest bathing, or immersing yourself in nature. The practice emerged in Japan and is called *shinrin-yoku*, which translates to forest bathing, where researchers studied the benefits of forest bathing and found what native cultures or those who spend a lot of time outdoors already knew: breathing fresh, clean air is good for us. Essential oils, referred to as phytoncides, are released into the air from trees and other plants and contribute to the positive effect of forest bathing. It can reduce stress, lower blood pressure and heart rate, and promote a feeling of overall comfort and well-being. Picking and tasting wild plants enhance this euphoric feeling.

PRACTICING FOREST BATHING

The practice of forest bathing is very simple. No special gear is needed. All you need is a natural environment where you can immerse yourself totally in nature. It doesn't even have to be a forest. One does not have to go to the forest to make contact with the natural world. A walk on a beach and inhaling the salt air from the sea, being near a waterfall, or just walking around your yard and garden is also a way to connect with nature. Engaging in any of these activities can give one a sense of well-being.

When you first enter into the forest or other natural environment, take a moment to pause and take a few deep breaths, long and slow. In doing so, clear your mind of idle chatter and focus on what is happening around you. Listen to the sounds, smell the air, and observe. Walk at a leisurely pace and practice awareness, letting your instincts take the lead.

Mindfulness

Mindfulness is a concept that can be applied to all aspects of life. This is especially true while foraging, which can lead us into areas that are truly wild and home to often dangerous creatures. Pay attention to your body sensations while foraging. An itch on your leg or arm may indicate that a tick is looking for a meal. Remove it before it gets a chance to bite in. Learn to recognize poison ivy. Be aware of plants that look like what you're harvesting but may be something that's not edible. Know what poisonous look-alikes grow in the same environment and avoid them.

Being aware and fully present while engaged in our daily activities or while foraging is a skill that can be developed. When foraging, stop periodically, look around, and listen. One of the primary means for developing awareness is through mindfulness meditation. In the outdoors, this involves attuning to nature by being aware of the surrounding sights, sounds, and smells.

Use the Senses (Organoleptics)

Organoleptics is a sensory exploration of the plant world. Becoming aware of the different types of plants and how to distinguish between them is the first step. Plants have individual personalities and energy fields. We rely on sight as our primary way of getting to know a plant. But we can also use our senses of smell, touch, and, in some cases, taste to become familiar with a plant.

OBSERVATION

Look for patches of color with varying shades of green. They will reveal the different types of plants.

TOUCH

Use your sense of touch to feel the texture of the leaf (be sure to identify poison ivy before doing this). Rub it to see if it is hairy, rough, or smooth.

SMELL

The nose knows. Roses have an ethereal smell, some wildflowers have a floral scent, and others smell sweet. Not all smells are pleasant. Some have a camphor smell, others are pungent, and some are musky.

TASTE

If you feel comfortable with the identity of the plant, use your sense of taste to see how it tastes and feels. The taste often confirms the identity or the species of a plant.

Journaling

Journaling is a great way to deepen your connection with nature and document your experiences in the plant world by focusing your attention and enhancing your powers of observation and awareness. Recording the plants in a particular area lets you know where you can go to harvest them when they are in season. If the timing is right and the plant is ready for harvesting, you will know to come back in future years.

There are several styles that can be used for journaling. The simplest one is the log journal where you record the date, time, location, weather, and list of species identified. Include a description of the habitat, whether it is in the sun or shade, type of soil, moisture, and other plants growing around it.

Look for signs of insects or other wildlife that may be feeding on the leaves or stems. Plants act as host plants for insects. A curled-up leaf is a clue that there may be a caterpillar or other insect or spider inside. Birds seek out the berries, often leaving the stems hanging empty. Deer graze on foliage.

VOUCHER SPECIMENS

Taking plant specimens and labeling and mounting them can be a good way to remember them. Plant material used to make medicine or natural products is often obtained from plants harvested in the wild. A voucher specimen is essential and usually includes a pressed, dried herbarium specimen with detailed collection data on how it was harvested along with processing and preparation techniques. This data serves as a record of the plant's true identity.

PLANT SKETCHING

Plant sketching is an excellent way to connect with a plant, especially if you're in an area where picking is not allowed. When sketching a plant, look for plant details that include type of leaf, their arrangement on the stem, flowers, fruits, whether it is growing alone or in a colony, and how abundant it is. Sniff the flowers to see if there is a scent or crush the leaf and smell it. If there are edible fruits, taste one. Taste varies among different plants.

References

Duke, J. A. (2007). *Herb-A-Day*. Virginia Beach, VA: Eco Images.

CHAPTER TWO

SUSTAINABLE FORAGING

Foraging Ethics   8

Foraging Habitats   8

The Forager's Garden   8

Foraging Ethics

If you take from the earth, you must give back to the earth. This attitude is important. You don't want to be the cause of a plant becoming rare or extinct because of overharvesting. Make an offering with whatever feels comfortable for you.

Begin by showing appreciation and respect. When approaching a plant, observe not only the plant but also its surroundings. Pick up any litter lying around the area. If unwanted weeds or vines are crowding out a particular plant, remove them and leave the area looking better than when you approached it. Look for signs of spraying from herbicides or pesticides or other possible pollutants in the area before harvesting.

Sustainable harvesting can benefit the plant if done conscientiously. Thinning out a patch of greens will enable more to grow. Picking edible berries allows the plant more energy to produce more berries. A good rule of thumb, if there is an abundance of a particular plant, is to pick what you need and leave some to reseed, some for wildlife, and the rest for the next group of foragers if it's not your land. If you only see small patches here and there, it's best to leave it to continue to grow.

Foraging Habitats

Choosing good foraging grounds is important. Places where plants are allowed to grow naturally without sprays or mowing soon become habitats for wild foods. If you don't have space around you, look for an abandoned lot, a hedgerow that has grown up at the edge of a field or forest, a meadow, or a swamp that hasn't been sprayed with pesticides. If it's private land, be sure to ask permission of the landowner.

Lightly traveled roads in the country present foraging opportunities. Make sure you are at least fifty feet from the road, depending on how well traveled it is. If possible, get permission from the landowner.

As with all things in nature, wild foods are seasonal. Each habitat contains characteristic plants that mature and ripen at different times of the year. And it's not the same year every year. You may get a bountiful harvest one year and get nothing the next year. And then there are the unexpected surprises that you don't expect to find. Always have a collecting bag with you for those rare moments.

The Forager's Garden

"The earth does not belong to man; man belongs to the earth."

—Chief Seattle, Suquamish and Duwamish chief

If we choose to use wild plants for food and medicine, we need to make sure they have a place to grow. We must become caretakers of our wild gardens. Just like a gardener tends to his garden, so must a forager tend to the wild garden.

A forager's garden has a different feel and appearance than most gardens. A forager's garden has no boundaries. It's where the wild things grow. Generally, there are no designated rows of the same plant, or if there is a row, it is filled with weeds.

Having wild plants growing in your immediate surroundings is more convenient and more likely to be harvested than if you have to travel to other areas to find them.

Creating your own wild food habitat in your backyard or garden is one way of making sure you have foraging grounds. Having wild edibles nearby allows you to watch and know when to harvest. If planned carefully, wild plants can provide food throughout the year. Space and an opportunity to grow are all they need, while conscientious harvesting techniques can ensure their return year after year.

CULTIVATING WEEDS

"A weed is a plant you don't want. Once you find a use for it, it's no longer a weed. It's one way of getting rid of your weeds."

—Jim Duke

Sometimes tending to the wild garden means weeding the weed patch and removing those plants that aren't used or needed. If uncertain as to a plant's identity, leave it until it blooms. Once it has flowered, it is much easier to identify. Use a wildflower guide  to identify it, then look up its uses, both edible and medicinal. Establishing an area to grow wild edibles is the first step. You can begin by turning the soil over and leaving it fallow, observing which plants come up naturally without actually planting anything. Thousands of tiny seeds lie dormant in the soil, waiting for the right conditions to germinate.

ANNUAL FLOWERS

Annuals are herbaceous plants that germinate as the soil begins to warm up. Soon after, they bloom and go to seed. These annuals represent the first stage of succession in the plant community and will eventually be replaced by another community over time.

BIENNIAL FLOWERS AND PERENNIAL FLOWERS

Biennials and perennials also emerge at this time. Ragweed, crabgrass, and foxtail grass are in the first stage of succession and will eventually crowd out and replace the annuals unless they are removed. Biennials germinate in the fall, grow through the winter, and in the spring send up a flower stalk, bloom, and go to seed. Perennials send up new growth in the spring from roots that have remained alive through the winter and come back year after year. Some perennials completely die back while others simply lose their leaves but retain the main stem. Some plants are short-lived perennials and will come back for several years and then die off.

EXPANDING THE WILD GARDEN

Take inventory of what is in your garden and what you want to grow. Observe what plants grow well in similar environments and collect seeds from those areas. In some cases, you may want to transplant from nearby areas, especially if the plants are in danger of being removed by development, logging, or some other reason.

SOWING SEEDS (*Giving and Receiving*)

Spring is when you want to sow any wild seeds that were harvested in the previous year. Think about what you want to harvest in the summer and fall. Look for areas where you would naturally find those plants and clear out spaces around them to scatter your seeds. You can also select small areas in your yard or garden and selectively plant your seeds. This is your opportunity to give back to the earth so that she can keep on giving.

MAINTENANCE

Even a wild garden requires a certain amount of maintenance. If unattended, by the second or third year, grasses and seedlings of woody plants move in and succession begins. Tree seedlings can be transplanted to other areas in the yard if space allows, or they can be dug up for special occasions and given away as free trees. If it is a meadow, mowing in the spring and fall will prevent succession and still provide an abundance of wild edibles.

CHAPTER THREE

BENEFITS OF FORAGING

Economic Benefits   12

Weed Control   12

Nutritional Fitness   12

Why am I out here picking these berries when I can go to the store and buy them? This is a question that many have thought or asked themselves while foraging. There is no single answer. The benefits are many and the reasons vary from one individual to the next.

Economic Benefits

Wild plants are free. For those who are on a limited budget, including wild plants in the diet reduces food costs.

Weed Control

If you are an organic gardener, you probably spend a lot of time pulling weeds. Many of the weeds being pulled have more nutritional value than the plants you are growing for food and can be added to your salad bowl or other dish. Control your weeds by eating them.

Nutritional Fitness

In the process of trying to become healthier individuals, we are discovering that the foods we eat and their nutritional value play an important role in how we feel and how susceptible we are to certain ailments. Herbal dietary supplements line the shelves of health food stores along with vitamins and minerals to help us achieve good health. A number of these herbs can be found in the wild and were used by our ancestors as food and medicine to prevent and cure disease.

Generally, wild plants have a higher concentration of vitamins and minerals as well as other compounds that contribute to our good health. They contain less water than their cultivated relatives. Including wild edible plants into your diet can provide much needed nutrients to maintain good health and prevent illness before it occurs. Each herb has chemical properties that protect the body in different ways.

CHAPTER FOUR

BOTANY BASICS

Plants to Avoid   14

Plant Features   15

Plant Families   17

References   17

Knowing how to identify plants is a prerequisite for harvesting them for food and medicine. One must be able to recognize them in their natural environment, know what their look-alikes are, and what makes each plant unique and different from those growing around them.

Vascular plants can be divided into groups: Monocots start with one seed leaf and have parallel veins in the leaves. The flower parts are in multiples of three. Dicots have two seed leaves and netted veins. The flower parts are in multiples of four or five or more.

Plants to Avoid

Not all plants are edible. However, the risk of being seriously poisoned from eating wild plants is quite small. Most poisonous plants just don't taste good. They are either very bitter, pungent, or even putrid. Become familiar with the poisonous plants that grow in your area as well as the poisonous look-alikes.

Poisonous also doesn't necessarily mean it will kill you. You may get nauseous, feel gastrointestinal discomfort, break out in a sweat, or have an allergic reaction if you've never eaten the plant before. There are a few exceptions. Poison and water hemlock are among the most serious. Both hemlocks are in the carrot family, which can look very similar to poison hemlock. Other poisonous plants to familiarize yourself with include the following:

BUTTERCUPS (Ranunculus spp.)
Waxy yellow flowers with five petals that bloom at the same time as wood sorrel, which is smaller, not waxy, but also has five yellow petals.

YELLOW JESSAMINE (Gelsemium sermpervirens)
Has a fragrant, yellow, tubular flower in the spring and is often mistaken for honeysuckle. Its flower nectar has been known to poison honeybees.

POISON IVY (Toxicodendron radicans)
Leaves of three, let it be. However, there are a number of wild plants that have three leaflets and are harmless. Look for the hairy vine.

VIRGINIA CREEPER (Parthenocissus quinquefolia)
Often confused with poison ivy. In fact, it does often grow mixed in with it, but Virginia creeper does not cause the contact dermatitis rash.

However, the small, purplish berries are toxic and should be avoided.

POKEBERRIES (Phytolacca americana)
Purplish berries contain toxic seeds. While the berries can be eaten, poisoning can result if the seeds are ingested.

POISON HEMLOCK (Conium maculatum)
Member of the carrot family and can easily be confused with wild carrot. Both have fernlike, finely divided leaves and white, flat-topped clusters of flowers. Wild carrot, often referred to as Queen Anne's lace in the second year when it blooms, has a red dot in the center. Poison hemlock has reddish or purple blotches on the stems.

WATER HEMLOCK (Cicuta maculata)
Grows in a similar environment as elderberry. Both have compound leaves and white flat-topped clusters of flowers. Water hemlock's leaves are tri-pinnately compound whereas elderberry leaves have five to seven leaflets.

How to Avoid Plant Poisoning

- Begin by learning to identify the plants around you that are poisonous. Look for those that may be a poisonous look-alike or are growing mixed in with edibles, disguised as an edible.
- Positive identification is a must. Sometimes just having green leaves isn't enough. Watch and wait for it to bloom. Wild plants are much easier to identify if they have flowers or fruits.
- Don't assume that because one part is edible the whole thing is edible. One plant can have poisonous, edible, and medicinal parts all on one tree.
- Practicing mindfulness is an important habit to develop. Be aware of what you are gathering, where it is growing, and what's growing around it. Poison ivy is common in most environments.

Keep in mind that the chances of becoming seriously poisoned from eating wild plants are quite small. Most plants that are poisonous taste poisonous. They are either very bitter, astringent, or even irritating sometimes. Your taste buds are a good guide.

Be aware of allergies. If you've never eaten a plant food before, whether it is wild or cultivated, you don't know that you're not allergic to it or that it's not going to affect you in an unpleasant way. An allergic reaction is not the same as being poisoned. Allergies are specific to individuals.

If you think a plant is edible but you're not absolutely certain, you can do a taste test. Start by placing a small morsel on your tongue and taste it. If it tastes bad, spit it out and wash your mouth out. If it tastes okay, put another small piece in your mouth, chew it up, roll it around on your tongue to get the full flavor, then swallow it. Wait ten to twenty minutes to see if there is any discomfort and if not, eat a small amount. Again, wait to see if it agrees with you.

Caution: This does not apply to mushrooms. Mushrooms can taste good going down but on day three you could start experiencing symptoms of being poisoned.

Plant Features

All plants have roots, stems, leaves, and will bloom and produce seeds when given the right conditions. Seeds are usually contained within a fruit and are dispersed in unique ways to grow new plants. Each plant part does something different.

ROOTS

Roots anchor the plant into the ground and absorb water and minerals from the soil that are transported to the stems and leaves. Extra food is stored in the roots.

- **Adventitious** roots extend out from the primary root and include rhizomes, stolons, tubers, and bulbs.
- **Bulbs** are underground stems with thickened, fleshy scales and include onions and garlic.
- **Corms** are vertical underground stems that are thickened but lack prominently

thickened leaves. These include arrowhead and arrow arum in the wild. Jack-in-the-pulpit has corms.

- **Rhizomes** are underground stems that grow horizontally and are usually fleshy and send out young shoots upward at the nodes, forming a colony. Cattails, sassafras, and pawpaw are examples.
- **Stolons** run horizontally over the ground and root at the tip, forming a new plant. Strawberries have stolons.
- **Taproots** are primary roots that originate from the seed. Examples of taproots include evening primrose, yellow dock, dandelion, and burdock.
- **Tubers** are thickened portions of rhizomes or roots that store food and nutrients and have nodes and buds. Groundnuts grow on a string and have enlarged portions along the string.

STEMS

Stems support the plant and provide conduits for transporting water and nutrients from the roots and leaves. Herbaceous stems are soft and flexible and bend easily whereas the stems of trees, shrubs, and some vines are woody and hard.

Stems have different textures. Herbaceous stems may be round, square, or triangular. Trees have a single stem and can be identified by their bark, even in the winter. The bark may be smooth, have ridges, shaggy, or have thorns. Shrubs have multiple stems. The stem color varies and may be light or dark. Some stems have a scent. Do the scratch and sniff test on a branch or twig to detect the scent.

- **Bark, twigs, and buds** also have individual characteristics that make them unique. Leaf buds are actually miniature leaves while the larger flower buds are miniature flowers. Usually, the flower buds are larger than the leaf buds.
- **Leaves** are where the plant's food is made. They capture the sunlight and through the process of photosynthesis make food that is transported to the rest of the plant. Leaves may be simple with a single leaf attached to the stem or compound with multiple leaflets.
  - **Type of leaf:** simple/compound

- **Leaf shape:** oval, lanceolate, triangular, circular
- **Texture:** rough, hairy, smooth, prickly
- **Leaf features:** entire, toothed, lobed
- **Leaf arrangement:** alternate, opposite, whorled

FLOWERS

The easiest time to identify plants is when they are in bloom. If the plant is in bloom, see what kind of flower it produces, its color, and the number of petals. Flowers often have a scent or are showy to attract pollinators.

Male versus Female Flowers

Distinguishing between male and female flowers is quite simple. Males have stamens and females have pistils. The stamen is the part that produces the pollen that is transported to the pistil by a pollinating insect or the wind. Sometimes the male and female flower parts are on the same flower, allowing for self-pollination. Other species have to be cross-pollinated even though they may have both sexes on one plant.

Once pollinated, the pollen travels down the tube of the pistil to the ovary where it fertilizes the egg. The fertilized egg begins to swell and develops into a fruit that will contain the seeds for the next generation.

Flower Types

- **Regular flowers:** All the flower parts are alike in size and shape.
- **Irregular flowers** have different shapes or sizes on the same flower.
- **Indistinguishable flowers:** Flowers that have no obvious petals or flower parts or are so small they can't be distinguishable.

Flowers grow in different arrangements and may take the form of a head, spike, raceme, umbel, or spadix:

- **Head:** A group of flowers joined together in a short, dense, terminal cluster.
- **Spike:** An elongated cluster of flowers without stalks along a central stem.
- **Raceme:** An elongated flower cluster with stalked flowers along a central stem.
- **Umbel:** A flower cluster with all flower stalks radiating from the same point.
- **Spadix:** A spike with small flowers on a fleshy stem.

FRUITS

Fruits contain the seeds, the lifeline of the plants. It is from the seeds that new life will emerge. Plants have developed unique features that provide the means for plants to disperse their seeds. These adaptations allow the plant to have a wider range of distribution.

Seed Dispersal

Many fruits contain seeds that simply drop to the ground under the parent plant and emerge as an abundance of tiny plants under the tree. Others have wings or parachutes that propel them through the air where they can ride the winds for a distance. Then there are the hitchhikers that attach themselves to animals and are dropped or rubbed off along the trail. Tasty fruits attract animals that eat the fruits and pass the seed through their digestive system where new plants will grow. Fruits may be fleshy or dry. If it is fleshy, it may be a berry, drupe, or pome.

Fleshy Fruits

Berries: Fleshy fruits with seeds distributed throughout. Blueberries, huckleberries, persimmons, grapes, passionfruits, and pawpaws are berries.

Drupes: Fleshy fruits with a single seed in the center, sometimes two. Wild cherries (*Prunus* spp.), plums (*Prunus* spp.), and black gum berries (*Nyssa sylvatica*) are examples of drupes.

Pomes: Fleshy fruits that have an outer wall and an inner paper, cartilage-like wall surrounding the seeds. Apples, crabapples, and hawthorns (all members of the Rose family) have pomes.

Dry Fruits

Dehiscent: Dry fruits that split along definite seams called sutures and include legumes, follicles, and capsules.

Legumes: Pods that crack open along two sutures and include members of the pea family.

Follicles: Fruits that develop from a single pistil and break along only one suture. Prickly ash (*Zanthoxylum* spp.) has follicles. The fruits are small and round and split open when mature to reveal a shiny, black seed.

Capsules: Fruits that develop from a compound pistil and may contain many seeds. An example is evening primrose (*Oenothera biennis*) with capsules that are green, then turn brown when they ripen, containing many little black seeds.

Indehiscent: Dry fruits do not split open and include achene, samara, and nuts.

Achenes: Small, one-seeded fruits that are hard and need to be split to release the seed. Sunflower seeds and strawberry fruits are achenes.

Nuts: Characterized by a single seed that is surrounded by a hard shell. Around the hard shell is a protective husk that can assume different shapes. The outer husk may be leafy, woody, or spiny. True nuts include acorns, black walnuts, chestnuts, hazelnuts, hickory nuts, and beechnuts.

Samaras: Fruits that have a thin, membrane-like wing with a seed attached on the end. Maples (*Acer* spp.), ash (*Fraxinus* spp.), and elm (*Ulmus* spp.) have samaras.

Plant Families

Plants have families and share common characteristics, including the flower type, number of petals, and leaf arrangement. Just because plants share similar properties and are in the same family doesn't always mean that they can all be used the same way. There may be edible, medicinal, and poisonous plants in the same family. This is why it's important to get to know an individual species before using it.

References

Elpel, T. (2006). *Botany in a day: The patterns method of plant identification*. Pony, MT: HOPS Press, LLC.

Harlow, W. H. (1946). *Fruit key & twig key to trees and shrubs*. New York: Dover Publications.

North Carolina State University. "Poisonous Plants." Retrieved from https://projects.ncsu .edu/cals/plantbiology/ncsc/poisonousplants .htm.

PART 2
FOLLOW THE SEASONS (PLANT CYCLES)

The seasons are influenced by changes in the climate. These changes require harmonizing with nature and using the plants that are available at that time of year. By following the natural cycles of plants, we get what we need when we need it.

CHAPTER FIVE
SPRING

Pollen   22

Allergies   22

Detoxification   22

Spring Greens   23

Spring Scents   24

Tree Sap   25

References   25

Spring is a joyful time. Early morning sounds of birds singing, the hum of insects, and the evening chorus of frogs are indicators that spring has sprung. The feeling of love is in the air as birds sing beautiful melodies to attract a mate and babies are emerging all around us in the animal world.

The arrival of spring brings with it longer daylight hours, warmer temperatures, and the stirring of life awakening from its winter slumber. Spring is a time of birth, renewal, and blossoming.

In the spring there is a sudden burst of growth from the plant world. It is a time when seeds are sprouting, buds are swelling, flowers are blooming, and sap is moving from the roots of trees to their branches followed by a bright coat of green as new leaves unfurl.

Pollen

With spring comes pollen. A layer of dust, often yellow, settles on the ground in puddles. Most of the pollen you see is primarily coming from pines. The time to harvest pine pollen is just before it reaches this stage.

Cattails also produce pollen that can be collected a little later in the spring. Watch for the male flower buds to start swelling and turning yellow. A slight tap on the stalk will let you know they're ready by releasing a cloud of yellow dust into the air.

Allergies

Allergies are often the result of imbalances and stress in our lifestyle and occur as an immune response to pollen, dust, mold, smoke, and other irritants that are in the air that we breathe. Allergic responses include coughing, sneezing, congestion, watery eyes, and runny nose. Often referred to as hay fever, these allergic reactions are the body's attempt to wash out these irritants and rid itself of particles trapped in the mucosal lining of the airways. Managing your stress level with the use of herbs can boost the immune system and help prevent an allergic response. Cleansing the body of toxins that have built up over the winter can also improve your resistance to allergens.

Detoxification

Spring has traditionally been considered a time to detox. Spring tonics are used to strengthen and cleanse the body of fats and heavy foods consumed through the winter. Plants that are available in the spring that can be used to detox the body include dandelions, cleavers, thistle,

---

Pollen Cakes

Use as a base for spreads and sauces.

- 3 eggs
- ½ cup butter, melted
- ¼ cup half-and-half
- 2 cups cattail pollen
- ¼ cup pine pollen
- 1 cup dandelion flowers
- 2 cups corn meal
- 2 tablespoons molasses
- ¼ cup hot water

Beat eggs. Add butter and half-and-half. In a separate bowl, mix pollen, dandelion flowers, and corn meal. Add to beaten egg mixture. Stir in molasses. Add hot water and mix. Drop by spoonfuls onto hot, oiled griddle. Cook until golden brown on each side.

Terms to Know

Adaptogens are substances that combat the negative effects of stress and improve our physical and mental endurance.

Alteratives are substances that stimulate the lymphatic system to drain fluids and toxins from the tissues; formerly referred to as blood purifiers.

Diuretics are substances that flush toxins from the kidneys and bladder by increasing urination.

Cholagogues are medical agents that promote the flow of bile from the gallbladder.

Choloretics are substances that stimulate the production of bile by the liver.

Corticoids are anti-inflammatory hormones.

Diaphoretics are substances that have the power to increase perspiration.

Laxatives are substances that cleanse the digestive system and colon.

---

mustard greens, yellow dock, burdock, poke, and roots of biennials before they bloom.

Detoxification is a therapeutic method of treating disease since ancient times. Most therapeutic methods focus on the colon, since it is the largest organ of detoxification, but other organs of detoxification include the skin, liver, gallbladder, intestines, lymphatics, kidneys, and bladder.

Spring Greens

Greens can be found in a variety of habitats, from the backyard to the fields, forests, marshes, and even swamps. Sometimes there is an overlap, but some greens require specific conditions to grow. Some will grow in the sun, while others like the shade. Regardless, greens can be found almost everywhere and at any time of the year, but early spring is when they are most abundant.

WILD MUSTARD (Brassica spp.)

Wild mustards are one of the most common weeds in the country. With more than four thousand species, it is one to know and use as food and food medicine. It blooms in the spring with four petals. The color ranges from white to yellow, and even lavender.

All species are edible and contain spicy, pungent-tasting compounds that are characteristic of the mustard family. Depending on the species, all parts can be eaten and act to stimulate digestion. The young leaves, flower buds, and seeds are all edible.

BURDOCK (Arctium spp.)
Burdock is a biennial and has a deep taproot that is used for detox by helping to eliminate metabolic wastes. It also stimulates the secretion of bile as well as other digestive enzymes. Burdock is a diuretic and an alterative, formerly referred to as a blood purifier.

YELLOW DOCK (Rumex crispus)
Yellow dock is a bitter herb that supports detoxification as a laxative and as an alterative. Young roots are gathered in the spring before they send up a flower stalk and used fresh to make tea or added to soup. They can also be dried for future use.

CLEAVERS (Galium aparine)
Cleavers work as a lymphatic cleanser and are only available in the spring.

STINGING NETTLE (Urtica dioica)
Stinging nettle is a diuretic and is nutritional, adding vitamins and minerals that are flushed out through detoxification.

THISTLE (Silybum marianum, Cirsium spp.)
Milk thistle is a well-known herb used to detox the liver. A number of thistles that grow wild can also be used the same way. All thistles are liver cleansers and are best harvested in the spring before the flower opens for the buds and stalks. Seeds are harvested later in the year.

Detox Soup
This is a warming and cleansing soup to have whenever you need a cleanse.

- 1 tablespoon coconut oil
- 5 cloves garlic, chopped
- 1 medium yellow onion, chopped
- 3 celery stalks, chopped
- 4 carrots, chopped
- 1 cup wild chives (*Allium* spp.), chopped
- 3 dandelions (*Taraxacum officinale*), leaves and roots, scraped and chopped
- 3 evening primroses (*Oenothera biennis*), leaves and roots, scraped and chopped
- 1 yellow dock (*Rumex crispus*), leaves and root, scraped and chopped
- 2 burdock (*Arctium minor*) roots, scraped and chopped
- 1 cup stinging nettle (*Urtica dioica*) leaves, chopped
- ½ teaspoon evening primrose (*Oenothera biennis*) seeds
- ⅛ teaspoon black pepper
- ⅛ teaspoon cayenne pepper
- ⅛ teaspoon sea salt
- ⅛ teaspoon turmeric
- 1 quart vegetable broth

Heat coconut oil in a large skillet on medium heat. Sauté the vegetables in order, allowing each one to meld before adding the next. Add remaining ingredients. Mix well. Cover and reduce heat to simmer for 20 to 30 minutes.

Spring Scents

"Smell is a potent wizard that transports us across a thousand miles and all the years we have lived."

—Helen Keller

Spring showers and freshly tilled earth bring back memories of a simple way of life for many people. The fragrant scent of flowers can affect the mood and emotions by triggering the production of hormones in the body that are uplifting and relaxing. Flowers have long been used as fragrances for perfumes, scented oils to beautify the body and soothe the spirit, and even as a source of food and medicine. Scents are therapeutic and can be used for relaxation, to ease depression, relieve nausea and headaches, and help to ease colds, congestion, and asthma. Scents can even be used to energize us.

EDIBLE FLOWERS

Some flowers are edible and can be used to add a decorative touch to salads or desserts. Flowers have a variety of tastes. Many flowers have a taste similar to their scent and range from spicy to sweet to almost no taste at all. How they are used is equally variable. Even though edible flowers can be harvested throughout the year from some plants, spring is when they are most abundant with the greatest diversity.

Wildflower Salad

A blend of wildflowers that can add color and nutrition to your meal.

- Dandelion flowers (*Taraxacum officinale*)
- Wild mustard (*Brassia* spp.)
- Redbud (*Cercis canadensis*)
- Violets (*Viola* spp.)
- Wild pansy (*Viola bicolor*)
- Wood sorrel (*Oxalis* spp.)
- Juice of 1 lemon
- Maple syrup

Toss flowers in a salad bowl. Combine lemon juice and maple syrup. Pour over flowers. Chill and serve.

Dandelion is one of the first wildflowers to bloom, beginning in late winter and continuing into the spring. These flowers are mildly sweet with a little bitterness. Members of the mustard family bloom at the same time. Their buds and flowers are both edible and come in an assortment of colors. These flowers are spicy and strong in taste and are best when used in salads or infused in vinegar. Sassafras flowers and buds are also pungent and mucilaginous and can be added to salads. Sassafras blooms in the early spring before the leaves have emerged.

About mid-spring, redbuds and violets burst into flower. These flowers are mildly sweet and make colorful toppings for dessert dishes. Wild roses are fragrant and the petals can be used to make flower water. Later in the summer other flowers become available and include elder, passionvine, various mints, and goldenrod. These are best used to make a tea or tincture.

Poisonous Flowers

Not all flowers are edible. As with any plant, make sure you know that a plant is edible before consuming. Know what the poisonous look-alikes are as well. Buttercups (*Ranunculus* spp.) have five yellow petals and are not edible. Wood sorrel (*Oxalis* spp.) also has five yellow petals but is edible.

Smell is not always a reliable indicator. Honeysuckle (*Lonicera japonica*) flowers are popular among children who like to sip the nectar from the flowers. There is a similar-looking plant referred to as "swamp honeysuckle" that is actually an azalea (*Rhododendron* spp.) and has fragrant flowers that are extremely toxic. Yellow Jessamine (*Gelsemium sempervirens*) has yellow, tubular flowers that have a honeysuckle appearance and sweet fragrance and have been mistaken for honeysuckle. The nectar from those flowers contains strychnine and has been known to poison honeybees (Kingsbury, 1965).

HARVESTING FLOWERS

Harvest flowers on a clear, dry day around mid-morning when they are reaching their peak in color and fragrance. Avoid picking those flowers that are wilted or have drooped. Remove the whole flower head when picking with little or no stem. Keep in the shade while picking. Lightly shake them to remove pollinating insects. When possible, leave flowers unwashed to retain the pollen and nectar.

Rose Petal Honey

Provides an ethereal taste to your tea or beverage.

- 1 ounce fresh rose petals
- 1 cup raw honey

Cover the rose petals with honey. Infuse for several days.

It's best to use fresh flowers when harvesting them for food or medicine. They begin to lose their potency once they have been picked. If you're not going to use them immediately, spread them out on a screen or rack. If you plan to use them as an oil infusion, let them wilt at least twenty-four hours before infusing with them.

Flower-Infused Water

Add ice for a refreshing summer drink to sip on.

Flowers contain the essence of the plant and can be infused with water. This can be done with a number of edible flowers that vary depending on the season. The best spring flowers are roses, violets, and honeysuckle. As summer approaches, various members of the mint family bloom and are excellent in water.

Collect flowers early in the morning with a pair of kitchen scissors before the dew has lifted. Fill a glass bowl or pitcher with non-chlorinated water. Clip the stems off your flowers of choice just below the head, being careful not to contaminate the flowers themselves. Place the flowers on the surface of the water and place in direct sunlight uncovered for at least three hours. Strain and drink.

Tree Sap

In the spring, tree sap begins to rise with nutrients that have been stored in its roots throughout the winter. It rises fast to the tops of trees and is watery and thin. This is when trees are tapped for sap to boil down for syrup. Spring is also the best time to harvest tree bark for medicinal purposes because the inner bark (used for medicine) is much easier to peel at this time of the year.

TEA TONICS

Tonics can also be made from different types of trees. Sassafras roots were traditionally used in the spring to cleanse the blood. Twigs of sweet birch and spicebush are decocted into a tea and combined with sassafras to produce a tasty tonic that is both strengthening and rejuvenating.

SSS Tonic

A blend of sassafras tea, spicebush, and sweet birch teas for a spring tonic.

- 12 medium sassafras roots
- 1 cup spicebush twigs, cut in ½-inch strips
- 1 cup sweet birch twigs, cut in ½-inch strips
- 1 quart water
- Honey or maple syrup to taste

Wash sassafras roots, being sure to leave the bark, because that's where the flavor is. Place roots and twigs in cold water in a pot. Bring to a boil. Reduce heat and continue to simmer for about an hour. The longer you cook it, the stronger it gets. If it's too strong, you can dilute it with more water. Sweeten with honey or maple syrup to taste.

References

Kingsbury, J. M. (1965). *Deadly harvest: A guide to common poisonous plants.* New York: Holt, Rinehart and Winston.

CHAPTER SIX

SUMMER

Heat and Hydration   28

Summer Berries   28

Summer Greens   29

Skin Protection   29

References   31

Heat and Hydration

Summer is a lazy time when the days are long and the heat can sometimes be stifling. The longer days of summer allow for more time outside for foraging, preserving the harvest while it's in season, maintaining garden beds, and doing more outdoor recreational activities.

Summer activities require a greater output of energy and body fluids in the form of perspiration. Our body's essential salt and minerals are lost in the sweating process. This can lead to headaches, achy muscles, nerve issues, and exhaustion, but cooling herbs can help us stay hydrated. Fortunately, nature has provided us with a number of herbs that are cooling and calming at a time when we most need them.

Summer Berries

I was awakened by the cackling sound of red-bellied woodpeckers outside my bedroom window and instinctively knew the red mulberries were ripening. Mulberries are one of the woodpecker's favorite foods at this time of year and I know if I want any I have to get out early. The tree in front of my house was loaded. I have an agreement with the woodpeckers. I pick from the lower branches and they can have the ones at the top where I can't reach. And so together we picked. The berry season had begun.

—Vickie Shufer, personal journal entry

At the hottest, driest time of the year, we get our sweetest, juiciest berries. This is the time when we need sugars for energy and fluids for the hot, dry days of summer. The fruits contain flavonoids that are cooling and refreshing. Unripe fruits are bitter and sour.

While hiking during the summer months, look for the berry patches. When it's hot and dry, water isn't enough. Berries are strengthening and blood-building. Wild fruits and berries contain lots of vitamins and minerals and have been referred to as nature's sugar. Blueberries, cherries, blackberries, and raspberries make great trail nibbles and are excellent mashed and added to water, making a quick juice drink that provides nutrients and antioxidants for dealing with the heat.

ELECTROLYTES

Electrolytes are minerals that not only regulate body functions but also help to maintain proper fluid balance. Adding electrolytes into your diet can hydrate your body more effectively. The most common electrolytes include calcium, potassium, magnesium, phosphorus, sodium, and chloride. During intense exercise or working outside, these electrolytes need to be replenished. Herbal teas, berries, juice drinks, and adaptogens can help.

Sumac-Ade

- 1 cup sumac berries, ground
- 4 cups cold water
- 1 tablespoon maple syrup

Infuse berries in cold water for 3 to 4 hours. Strain and sweeten with maple syrup.

Herbal Electrolyte Drink
A simple electrolyte drink to replenish much-needed minerals after working out.

- 2 cups sumac-ade (recipe above)
- 1 fresh lemon, squeezed
- 2 tablespoons blueberry or elderberry syrup
- ⅛ teaspoon salt
- ½ cup sparkling water

Combine ingredients. Serve over ice and drink as needed to replenish energy.

COOLING HERBAL TEAS

Drinking cooling herbal teas is a great way to add fluids and minerals to the body. Natural diaphoretics stimulate sweating, which releases heat from the body. Elderflower and yarrow are natural diaphoretics that become available in late spring and early summer as the days are starting to heat up. Adding peppermint or lemon balm to these diaphoretic teas increases their cooling effect and taste. Adding a sweetener such as honey, maple syrup, or organic cane sugar contributes flavor, nutrients, and energy.

Summer Flower Tea

*A colorful and cooling tea
for the summer months.*

- 1 cup evening primrose flowers
- 2 cups beebalm flowers
- 10 echinacea flowers
- ½ cup oxeye daisy flowers
- 5 sprigs peppermint flowering tops

Pick flowers in the morning after the dew has lifted and put in a clear pitcher with cold water. Place in the sun for several hours. Strain and drink.

Sumac (*Rhus* spp.)
Sumac berries ripen at different times, depending on the species, beginning in mid-summer. They should be harvested when they are at their peak and before a rain. The fruits are sour and cooling and can be made into a refreshing drink.

Mallow (*Hibiscus* spp.)
Mallow plants begin blooming in mid-summer and should be harvested as the buds begin to swell. They can be infused in water for a cooling drink.

Passionvine (*Passiflora incarnata*)
The fruits of the passionvine are sour and sweet. The leaves, flowers, and stems can be brewed to make a calming and relaxing tea.

Summer Cooler

This is a refreshing tea that is cooling to drink on a hot summer day. This recipe is best prepared as a cold-water infusion the night before serving.

- ½ cup mallow root, chopped
- 1 teaspoon lemon balm leaves and flowers
- ¼ cup sumac berries
- 1 teaspoon lemon verbena leaves
- 1 cup linden flowers
- Cold water

Add herbs to quart jar and cover with cold water. Infuse overnight. Strain and drink.

Wild Berry Syrup (with sugar)

- 1 cup organic cane sugar
- 2 cups berries such as serviceberries, blueberries, mulberries, blackberries, or cherries

Add sugar to berries in a saucepan and bring to a boil. Continue to cook for five minutes. Pour into a sterilized jar and seal.

Wild Berry Syrup (with honey)
Add honey to the berries and heat on medium-low heat, not to exceed 110°F, until the honey has blended well with the fruit or juice. Do not simmer or boil. High temperatures will denature the honey (Cech, 2000).

Summer Greens
Purslane, lambsquarters, and amaranth are all heat-loving plants that come up in late spring and early summer and serve as a great source of summer greens.

Purslane-Tomato Salad

*A cool, refreshing salad
for the hot days of summer.*

- 2 cups purslane, chopped
- 3 Juliette or Roma tomatoes, chopped
- 1 cayenne pepper, chopped
- 1 teaspoon honey
- Salt to taste
- 3 tablespoons garlic vinegar (or other mustard vinegar)
- 3 tablespoons chives, chopped

Combine purslane, tomatoes, pepper, and honey. Add salt to taste and pour garlic vinegar on top. Garnish with chives. Chill and serve.

Skin Protection
With warmer temperatures and more time spent outdoors comes the need to protect the skin. There are a number of herbs that can be infused in a fixed oil to make salves and lotions

for moisturizing the skin and protecting it from poison ivy, insects, and to relieve itching. Sweet almond oil, olive oil, and grapeseed oil are fixed oils that can be used to make herbal infusions.

spp.). This is your sting relief. The leaves are edible so you can comfortably make a spit poultice by chewing on the leaves to moisten them, then applying them directly to the sting. Within minutes, the sting should disappear.

Rosemary-Mint Body Butter
A moisturizing butter to use on dry skin or hands.

- ½ cup peppermint-infused oil
- ½ cup rosemary-infused oil
- ¼ cup coconut oil
- 2 ounces shea butter
- 1½ ounces beeswax, cut in small pieces
- 10 drops rosemary essential oil
- 10 drops peppermint essential oil

Combine the peppermint-infused, rosemary-infused, and coconut oils. Add shea butter and beeswax. Heat in a double boiler until the shea butter and beeswax melt. Turn off heat and add the rosemary and peppermint essential oils. Pour into containers and let cool.

POISON IVY/POISON OAK/POISON SUMAC
Poison ivy, poison oak, and poison sumac are all members of the cashew family and can cause a contact dermatitis reaction among some people. Jewelweed (*Impatiens capensis*) works as an antidote and as a treatment for poison ivy. It blooms during the summer months, then goes to seed and dies back in the fall. Jewelweed is a native impatiens that is naturally juicy and can be crushed and applied fresh to the exposed or affected area.

Caution
Jewelweed is toxic to ingest so avoid doing a spit poultice when treating poison ivy/poison oak/poison sumac.

INSECT BITES AND STINGS
Insect activity is at its peak in the summer months. Wasps, bees, and hornets are easily provoked and inflict a painful sting. If this happens, look around for plantain (*Plantago*

Rid Itch Salve

- Yarrow (*Achillea millefolium*)
- Chickweed (*Stellaria media*)
- Plantain (*Plantago major, P. lanceolata*)
- Violet (*Viola sororia*)
- 1 cup sweet almond oil
- ¼ cup grated beeswax
- 10–20 drops lavender essential oil

Cover leaves with sweet almond oil and chop in a blender. Pour into a jar and place in a double boiler. Add water to the rim of the jar. Heat on low temperature for one hour. Let cool. Strain oil through a muslin cloth. Place oil and grated beeswax in a double boiler and heat until beeswax has melted. Add lavender essential oil to the salve and pour into containers to harden.

STINGING NETTLE (*Urtica dioica*)
There is a native species of nettles and an introduced species. Both will sting upon contact. If you're walking through the forest in the summer wearing shorts and your legs start stinging, look around. You have probably passed a nettles patch. Yellow dock (*Rumex crispus*) is the best remedy for nettle stings. The leaves are edible. A spit poultice of yellow dock leaves applied to nettle stings works great.

INSECT REPELLENT
Prevention is the best medicine for insect bites and stings. Depending on where you live, there are a number of herbs that can be used to repel insects. Aromatic herbs including mint species can be crushed and rubbed on the skin to act as a natural insect repellant. If you live along the coast where biting flies are numerous in the summer months, beautyberry (*Callicarpa americana*) and wax myrtle (*Morella cerifera*) are some of the most common coastal herbs to crush and use topically to prevent bites and stings.

The soap you use can also determine whether you are attracting or repelling insects. A favorite to use among foragers is made with pine tar. It is best to use it before going out into the field and again when you return. Pine tar soap also helps to prevent poison ivy if you bathe with it immediately after being exposed to it.

Herbal Insect Repellent

- ⅓ cup beautyberry tincture (leaves infused in vodka)
- 1 cup beautyberry oil (leaves infused in sweet almond oil)
- ½ peppermint oil (leaves infused in sweet almond oil)
- ½ cup lemongrass oil (leaves infused in sweet almond oil)
- ½ cup aloe water
- ⅓ cup witch hazel extract
- ⅓ cup rose petal tincture
- 10 drops peppermint essential oil
- 10 drops lemongrass essential oil

Combine all ingredients. Shake well. Apply liberally to skin.

References

Cech, R. (2000). *Making Plant Medicine*. Williams, OR: Horizon Herbs.

CHAPTER SEVEN

AUTUMN

Fall Cleansing   34

Allergies and the Immune System   34

Nuts   35

Bark   35

Saving Seeds   35

References   35

As summer winds down, there is a noticeable change in the decreased sunlight and cooler nighttime temperatures. In the plant world, leaves begin changing colors and dropping to the ground and nutrients are descending to the roots for storage. Life begins to slow down. There's a feeling of change in the air.

Fall Cleansing

Fall is a time of cleansing to prepare the body's immune system for the coming cold season and to support the slowing down process of the body's systems. Heartier foods are needed to supply us with greater energy for the cooler weather coming. Fall is also the time of year to dig for edible roots that can be used to make warming soups and teas. Roots that are available in the fall include burdock, yellow dock, dandelion, evening primrose, groundnuts, field garlic, and wild onions.

Dried Detox Soup Blend

An instant, healthy soup to warm you on a cold day.

- 2 quarts water or vegetable broth
- ¼ cup dried dandelion roots
- ½ ounce dried burdock roots
- 5 grams mallow root
- 10 grams dried dandelion leaves
- 1 teaspoon ground fennel seed
- 5 grams dried onion flakes
- 5 grams garlic granules
- ⅛ teaspoon turmeric
- 1 teaspoon evening primrose seeds, crushed
- 1 teaspoon wild mustard seeds
- Black pepper to taste
- Cayenne pepper to taste
- Salt to taste

Bring the water or vegetable broth to a boil. Add remaining ingredients. Reduce heat and cook for 30 minutes. Serve over rice if desired.

Allergies and the Immune System

Fall is a time when many allergens are released into the air. They can be inhaled, ingested, or simply come in contact with the skin. Allergies are the immune system's response to allergens and are often the result of an imbalance in our lifestyle. Any exogenous material including pollen, chemicals, and foreign bodies can trigger a reaction. Reducing stress levels and boosting the immune system can be supported with the use of herbs.

Immuni-Tea

A tea to boost the immune system for the coming allergy season.

- 20 grams dried elderflowers
- 15 grams dried echinacea flowers
- 10 grams dried lemon balm
- 10 grams dried sweet goldenrod leaves and flowers
- 5 grams dried pineapple sage
- Honey to taste

Mix herbs together. Add 1 cup hot water to 5 grams herb mix. Steep 10 to 15 minutes. Strain and sweeten with honey to taste.

Histamine is released as an immune response and often results in sneezing, itchy eyes, and a runny nose. Antihistamines prevent or inhibit the action of histamine and reduce the production of excess mucus. Nettles (*Urtica dioica*) and elder (*Sambucus canadensis*) provide natural antihistamines and can be taken in the form of a tea or tincture.

Allergy symptoms such as congestion, hay fever, headaches, and watery eyes also result from the release of histamine. Expectorants thin the mucus and strengthen the cough reflex. This helps to relieve congestion and expel mucus from the lungs or throat. Natural expectorants include wild black cherry, mullein, mallow, plantain, goldenrod, and beebalm and can be taken in the form of a tea or tincture.

Sneeze Arrest

Drink at the first sign of a sniffle or sneeze to relieve allergies or cold symptoms.

- 2 tablespoons goldenrod flowers and leaves
- 1 teaspoon nettles
- 2 tablespoons life everlasting
- 1 teaspoon elder flowers
- 1 teaspoon mullein leaves
- 1 teaspoon peppermint leaves and flowers
- 1 quart water

Combine herbs. Heat water to boiling and pour over herbs. Let steep 10 to 15 minutes. Strain and drink as needed throughout the day.

Nuts

The time to begin looking for nuts is in the fall, as the leaves begin to change color and drop to the ground. Nuts should be gathered as they drop and can be stored for future use. They can then be shelled as needed and used throughout the winter months. Most nuts are sweet, high in protein, and can be used as a substitute for meat in the diet. They are also rich in unsaturated fats that give them a high caloric value but no cholesterol.

Acorns (*Quercus* spp.) have a cap for an outer husk. Black walnuts (*Juglans nigra*) have an outer husk that looks like a smooth, green ball. Chestnuts (*Castanea pumila*) have needle-sharp spines surrounding the shell. Hazelnuts (*Corylus americana, C. cornuta*) have a leafy outer husk. Hickory nuts (*Carya* spp.) have an outer husk that splits open when mature. Beechnuts (*Fagus grandifolia*) have a triangular husk with weak spines.

Bark

Bark can be gathered in the fall or spring when the sugars and nutrients are either ascending or descending to the roots.

WILD CHERRY (*Prunus serotina*)
Wild cherry bark is anti-tussive; a tincture from the bark suppresses coughing and is used to treat asthma, bronchitis, and other respiratory conditions (Wood, 2009).

PRICKLY ASH (*Zanthoxylum clava-herculis*)
Also referred to as the toothache tree due to its numbing action, this bark can be peeled, dried, and prepared as a tincture or mouthwash.

Saving Seeds

Fall is the harvest season. You can collect seeds from edible plants growing around you or from areas where it's okay to collect seeds. Native seeds and/or plants are also available commercially. Rescuing plants from areas targeted for development is another way to obtain them. When harvesting, be sure to leave plenty to reseed for next year's growth (and don't forget to leave a few for the birds). Seeds need to be protected from heat, moisture, and light, so store your herbs in paper bags because plastic will produce mold. Thorough air-drying after seeds are collected is important and can be accomplished by hanging your paper bag(s) in a well-ventilated area. Once seeds are completely dry, they should be stored in a cool, dry place.

References

Wood, M. (2009). *The earthwise herbal: A complete guide to new world medicinal plants.* Berkeley, CA: North Atlantic Books.

CHAPTER EIGHT

WINTER

Winter Greens	38
Winter Teas	38
Winter Berries	38
Respiratory Health	39
Mood Elevators	40
Tree Talk	41
References	41

Winter is the end of all seasons. It is a time to seek inner warmth, rest, meditate, and replenish physical energy. Trees have dropped their leaves, exposing their buds and winter fruits. Foods are heavier and, in a hunting/gathering society, the time when wild game was hunted and brought to the table. Roots, nuts, and seeds that have been gathered and dried in the fall provide protein, fats, and calories for us through the winter months.

Leaves drop to the ground, vines hang limply, and meadows once again become user-friendly as grasses and second year perennials die back. However, this nonliving appearance is just an illusion. The plants are very much alive and all it takes is a little digging beneath the surface to realize this is true. In colder climates this may not be possible unless there is a warm spell and the ground begins to thaw. But for those who live in mild climates, there is lot of food just beneath the surface. Winter is the time to dig up edible roots and gather winter greens such as cresses and corn salad before they bloom and go to seed.

Winter Greens
Cool weather plants thrive in the winter. Springing up around dead stalks from the previous season's perennial grasses and wildflowers are winter greens. Cresses, wild mustards, corn salad, and sheep sorrel are the most abundant, with multivitamins that are needed to boost the immune system for the winter season.

Winter Teas
In the winter, we need inner warmth to warm the core and cool the surface. Teas, tinctures, and hot vinegar drinks bring the body heat deeper and lower. Pines are evergreen and easy to recognize by their needle-like leaves and are a good source of vitamin C. Pine needle tea can be used for respiratory infections.

Pine Needle Cough Syrup
A syrup to ease the cough.

- ½ cup pine needles, chopped
- 1 tablespoon sumac powder
- 1 cup water
- ½ cup honey

Add pine needles and sumac powder to water. Bring to a gentle boil. Lower heat and continue to simmer for 20 minutes. Remove from heat and add honey. Take as needed to ease coughing.

Hot Cider
A tea to warm you on a cold winter day.

- 1 quart apple cider
- 8 ginger slices
- 1 cinnamon stick
- Spicebush twigs

Place all ingredients in a slow cooker and heat for several hours.

Winter Berries
There are a number of wild fruits including rose hips and hawthorn that can be harvested during the winter months. These fruits are harder and less sweet than summer fruits and are decocted to make a tea that is high in vitamin C.

Hot Mulled Apple Cider with Rose Hips and Cranberry
A warming drink to enjoy for the holidays.

- 3 tablespoons dried rose hips
- 4 cups hot water
- 3 cinnamon sticks
- ½ teaspoon whole cloves
- 4 cups apple cider
- 2 cups cranberry juice
- 1 orange, sliced thin
- Cinnamon sticks for garnish if desired

Steep rose hips in hot water for 10 minutes, then strain. Transfer all ingredients to a large saucepan. Simmer on low for at least 1 hour before serving. Serve in festive mugs with a cinnamon stick as a garnish.

Rose Hip Tea

A drink high in vitamin C to boost the immune system for the winter.

- 1½ tablespoons fresh rose hips
- 1 quart water, divided
- 1 tablespoon maple syrup or agave nectar to taste

Blend rose hips with 1 cup water. Add remaining water and bring to a boil. Reduce heat and simmer for 20 to 30 minutes. Sweeten with maple syrup or agave nectar if desired.

Rose Hip Tincture

- 1 cup rose hips
- 2 cups water
- ¼ cup honey
- 1 cup apple jack brandy

Chop rose hips in blender. Place rose hips and water in a pot and bring to a gentle boil. Lower heat and continue to simmer until the liquid has reduced by half. Add honey and mix thoroughly. Add apple jack brandy, cover, and store for at least two weeks.

Respiratory Health

Winter is considered cold and flu season. Maintaining a healthy immune system is the first line of defense against colds and flus associated with colder weather. Herbs can be used to support the immune system naturally. Use wild herbs such as elderberries (*Sambucus canadensis*) and sumac (*Rhus* spp.) to make an immune-boosting tea.

Black Cherry Bark Syrup

A natural cough suppressant.

- 3 ounces fresh cherry inner bark
- 1 quart cold water
- 1 ounce simple syrup (mix equal parts sugar and water and heat until sugar is dissolved)
- 4 ounces grain alcohol

Combine cherry bark and water and bring to a boil, then reduce heat and continue to simmer until the liquid has reduced by half. Add simple syrup and grain alcohol. Take as needed to suppress coughing.

Respirade

Supports the respiratory system.

- ½ cup blueberry (*Vaccinium* spp.) cordial
- ½ cup elderberry (*Sambucus canadensis*) syrup
- ¼ cup black cherry (*Prunus serotina*) cordial
- ⅛ cup black cherry (*Prunus serotina*) bark syrup
- ⅛ cup osha root (*Ligusticum* spp.)

Combine ingredients. Take 1 tablespoon as needed for coughing.

STRESS MANAGEMENT

Reducing stress can alleviate symptoms or prevent the onset of symptoms associated with colds and flus. Managing your stress levels through the use of calming, relaxing herbs either as a tea or tincture can help promote a restful sleep.

CONGESTION

Coughing, sneezing, and tearing are nonrespiratory movements that keep the respiratory tract clear of irritants such as dust, pollen, or smoke. Nasal passages and sinuses are lined with mucus membranes that trap these irritants. If there is an insufficient amount of mucus, the result is a dry cough and can result in congestion or bronchitis. Cooling, moistening herbs include mallow, plantain, and violet. Expectorants are needed for hot, dry coughs and include elderflower, horsemint, beebalm, and mullein. Usnea can also be used for the respiratory system (Hoffman, 2003).

Cough-Ease

Helps relieve bronchial spasms and soothe respiratory airways. This tea is best prepared in the morning as a cold-water infusion.

- 1 tablespoon spearmint leaves and flowers
- 1 tablespoon beebalm leaves
- 1 tablespoon plantain leaves
- 1 teaspoon mullein leaves
- 1 teaspoon pineapple sage leaves and flowers
- 1 teaspoon violet leaves

Put herbs in a quart jar. Cover with cold water and let infuse for several hours. Strain and sip throughout the day.

Cold-Care

This is a great tea to sip on to help relieve allergies or when feeling the beginnings of a cold.

- 2 tablespoons goldenrod leaves and flowers
- 1 teaspoon peppermint
- 1 tablespoon beebalm flowers and leaves
- 1 teaspoon pineapple sage
- 1 teaspoon anise hyssop

Combine herbs. Add 1 tablespoon dried herbs per 1 cup hot water. Steep 10 to 15 minutes and drink.

Hi-C Drink

Boost your immune system with this drink that is rich in vitamin C and flavor.

- 2 tablespoons rose hips
- 2 tablespoons hawthorn berries
- 2 cups water
- ½ cup fresh pine needles, chopped
- 1 tablespoon hibiscus flowers
- Honey to taste

Simmer rose hips and hawthorn berries in 2 cups water for 30 minutes. Remove from heat. Add pine needles and hibiscus flowers. Cover and let steep for 10 to 15 minutes. Strain. Sweeten with honey to taste.

Mood Elevators

Shorter daylight hours and longer nights affect some people during the winter months. This affect is referred to as seasonal affective disorder (SAD) and is a type of depression. Adaptogens and calming herbs can help. St. John's wort and lemon balm, as a tea or tincture, can help relieve symptoms of SAD. Serotonin is known as a mood elevator. Black walnuts are one of the best sources of serotonin in the country. Evening primrose seeds are high in tryptophan, an amino acid that is used by the body to make serotonin.

B-Happy

A blend of tinctures to boost the mood during the short days of winter. This recipe yields 1 ounce.

- Lemon balm: 10 milliliters
- Linden: 9 milliliters
- St. John's wort: 5 milliliters
- Rose: 4 milliliters
- Mimosa: 2 milliliters

Combine all ingredients. Add a dropper of tincture to your tea or water or take as is.

Tree Talk

"On the banks, on both sides of the river, there will grow all kinds of trees for food. Their fruit will be for food, and their leaves for healing."
—Ezekiel 47:12

Trees provide food and medicine. The bark is the hard, outer layer that protects the tree from injury and insect invasion. Underneath that woody layer is another layer, referred to as the inner bark or phloem. It is through the inner bark of the branches, trunks, and roots that the sap containing the food material that is manufactured in the leaves is distributed (Grimm, 1962).

Winter is an excellent time to get to know your local trees. This is when you can see the skeleton of the forest because tree trunks, bark, and leafless branches stand out in the landscape. Even without leaves, trees can be identified by their bark, growth pattern, twigs, buds, and fruits, which on many trees mature in the winter and linger on until spring. The smooth, light-colored bark of beech trees is a sharp contrast to the dark ridges of oaks.

In the winter, it's easy to distinguish between the evergreen trees that keep their leaves all year and the deciduous trees that drop their leaves in the fall. Some trees hang on to their leaves even though they have turned yellow or even brown. Some evergreens have needle-like leaves while others have oval-shaped leaves.

References

Grimm, W. C. 1962. *The book of trees for positive identification*. New York: Hawthorn Books, Inc.

Hoffman, D. (2003). *Medical herbalism: The science and practice of herbal medicine*. Rochester, VT: Healing Arts Press.

PART 3
FOOD "FARM"ACY

"One of my main missions in life has been to bring herbs back into people's homes as more of a food and preventive medicine rather than when we're sick."
—Rosemary Gladstar, herbalist

CHAPTER NINE

KITCHEN LAB

Green Cuisine	46
Berries	46
Legumes	47
Roots	48
Nuts	49
References	49

The kitchen is where the magic happens. It is the place where the plain and ordinary can become something tasty and delightful. The kitchen is like the chemistry lab where you mix, measure, and combine plants that have thousands of phytochemicals, add a few ingredients to enhance the flavor and texture, and hope for the best. The results can be amazing. It is especially fun to create your own recipes using wild ingredients. Keep a record of what you make so that you can go back and repeat the same experiment.

Green Cuisine

Greens are purifying and provide us with necessary vitamins and minerals that should be a part of our daily diet. They boost the immune system and can be used to treat common ailments. Green plants are able to make their own food. They contain a pigment called chlorophyll that can capture the sunlight and through the process of photosynthesis make food that can be consumed by other life forms. Chlorophyll contains carbon, hydrogen, oxygen, and nitrogen grouped around a single atom of magnesium. Light energy turns into chemical energy. Chlorophyll stops the spread of bacteria, fungi, and other microorganisms and promotes the growth of beneficial intestinal flora (Pitchford, 2002).

Wild Herb Spread

A tasty spread that is packed with nutrition.

- 2 cups fresh wild greens (bittercress, peppercress, wild chives, corn salad)
- 4 ounces goat cheese
- 4 ounces cream cheese

Put all ingredients in a food processor and blend. Serve on crackers or bread.

MICROGREENS

Microgreens are just what they sound like: miniature greens. When an edible green produces seeds, hundreds of tiny plants come up around it. This includes corn salad (*Valerianella* spp.) and members of the mustard family. Microgreens fall between a sprout and baby leaf vegetables. The flavor is intense with concentrated nutrients.

BACKYARD GREENS

The best place to begin looking for wild greens is in your backyard during the spring. Many of the weeds that come up in our yards and gardens are edible greens. They also come up in the cracks of sidewalks, at the edges of parking lots, and any spot where there is bare soil. Many are referred to as invasive aliens and efforts are made to eradicate them, but these same weeds that we fight to get rid of are loaded with vitamins and nutrients and are often more nutritious than the cultivated vegetables they are growing next to.

Wild Herb Seasoning

A blend of dried herbs to add flavor and nutrition to any dish.

- ½ cup nettles
- ½ cup garlic mustard leaves
- 2 tablespoons chives
- ¼ cup field garlic/wild onions, chopped
- ¼ cup bittercress leaves
- ½ cup peppercress leaves
- 1 teaspoon wild mustard seeds
- 1 tablespoon pine pollen

Combine all ingredients in a grinder or food processor and blend. Use as a seasoning on vegetables, salads, and soups.

Berries

Berries are nature's sugars and can be used as a natural sweetener in many recipes, either as a substitute for sugar or to reduce the amount being used. Berries are blood building and strengthening. Dark-colored berries contain compounds known as anthocyanocides that contribute to visual acuity. Anthocyanocides also offer protection against ulcers by stimulating the production of mucus that protects the stomach lining (Duke, 1997).

Berry Bites

A tiny morsel of sweetness for extra energy.

- ⅔ cup butter
- 1 cup organic cane sugar
- 1 teaspoon vanilla extract
- 2 eggs
- ⅔ cup nut milk
- 2 cups oats
- 2 cups flour
- ⅔ cup wild blueberries
- ⅔ cup shelled nuts

Cream together butter and sugar. Stir in vanilla and add eggs and nut milk. Add oats and flour. Fold in berries and nuts. Drop by spoonsful on an oiled baking sheet. Bake at 350°F for 10 to 15 minutes. Cool and serve.

JUICES

Cooking with berries often involves extracting the juice. This can be done by heating the fruit in a saucepan with just enough water to cover the fruit for about 15 minutes. Once the juices start flowing, strain through a food mill or sieve to separate the juice and pulp from the seeds. A steam juicer works well when working with a large quantity and is especially good for cherries, grapes, black gum fruits, and other fruits with small seeds that cling to the pulp.

Black Cherry Juice

A strengthening juice to drink on a hot summer's day.

- 2 cups cherries
- ¼ cup water
- Maple syrup or other sweetener to taste

Place cherries in a saucepan. Add water and heat just to point of boiling. Lower heat to medium and cook 10 to 15 minutes longer. Use a food mill, sieve, or strainer to separate the juice from the seeds. Add maple syrup or other sweetener if desired. Drink as is or with sparkling water to give it a fizz.

WILD JELLIES, JAMS, AND JUICES

Making jelly, jam, or juice out of wild fruits is one way of preserving the fruit and enjoying it year-round. The process is simple and can be done with little effort or expense. Some wild fruits are better for making jelly than others. Wild grapes contain natural pectin, especially in the unripe state, and will jell without commercial pectin. Other fruits high in pectin include blackberry, black gum, cranberry, crabapples, rose hips, and hawthorn. Pawpaw, persimmon, sumac, blueberry, and elderberry are among those that are low in pectin. Combining these fruits with those that are high in pectin is one way to ensure that they will jell. Another way of making jelly is to add commercial pectin, either in the liquid or granular form. Liquid pectin can be made from the juice of crabapple and hawthorn or other fruits that are high in pectin.

Wild Grape Jelly

- 4 cups wild grapes
- ½ cup water
- 2 cups sugar

Bring grapes and water to a boil for 5 to 10 minutes, until the grapes are soft. Extract the juice by processing through a food mill. Add the sugar and bring to a rapid boil for about 10 minutes until the mixture forms a gel-like consistency. Pour into hot, sterilized jars and seal.

FRUIT SYRUPS

Fruit juices, cooked with a sweetener, make syrups that can be used as a food or medicine. For each pint of juice, add a cup of honey. Cook on medium-low heat 10 to 20 minutes until the mixture is somewhat thickened.

Legumes

Legumes are pea-like plants that are easily recognized in the wild because of their close resemblance to the many cultivated varieties of beans and peas. There are many species of legumes scattered throughout the world that consist of trees, shrubs, herbs, and vines.

A common trait of all species of the legumes family is a pod that releases its seeds by splitting open along two seams. Many of these seeds and pods are poisonous, especially when eaten raw. However, there are also a number of legumes that have edible seeds and/or pods that are edible but must be cooked first to destroy the lectins that are widespread in this family. Lectins can impair tissue functions and are potentially toxic. Processing and cooking destroy lectins in foods.

Poisonous Legumes

- Lupines (*Lupinus* spp.)
- Black locust (*Robinia pseudoacacia*)
- Rosary pea (*Abrus precatorius*)
- Locoweed (*Astragalus* spp. and *Oxytropis*)

REDBUD (*Cercis canadensis*)

When the redbud tree blooms, you know that spring has arrived. The flowers appear in conjunction with the mating calls of songbirds and chorus of frogs in the ponds and swamps. Soon after it has finished flowering, the pods develop. It's the young pods that are edible and can be cooked like snow peas.

WILD BEANS (*Strophostyles* spp. and *Phaseolus polystachios*)

Wild beans are ancestors of our cultivated beans and closely resemble each other except for a few technicalities. Both plants are climbing vines with compound leaves consisting of three-five leaflets. The fruit is a bean-like pod that is very similar to our garden beans.

The genus *Strophostyles* grows in the eastern part of the United States and has flowers and fruits that grow in small clusters. The pod, which develops in late summer and early fall, can be cooked like green beans when very young. Once the seeds have developed, the pod becomes too tough to eat, but the seeds can be shelled and eaten as beans.

Phaseolus polystachios is available along the Mississippi and Ohio rivers and the Gulf and Atlantic coastal plains. The seedpods develop in late summer and early fall and resemble green beans and can be cooked the same way.

Wild Bean Salad

- 1 cup cooked wild beans
- ¼ small red onion, chopped
- 1 tablespoon field garlic vinegar
- 1 tablespoon fig balsamic vinegar
- 1 medium red pepper, chopped
- 1 tablespoon wild onion vinegar
- 1 cayenne pepper, chopped
- 1 teaspoon zest seasoning

Combine all ingredients and marinate for 1 hour before serving.

Roots

Roots gather in the fall and into the winter and spring before sending up flower stalks. This is when most of the plant world is preparing for its winter slumber. Nutrients are descending to the roots growing beneath the surface where they absorb and store food, water, and minerals. Look for wild roots in gardens, meadows, and wetlands.

SOUPS

Soups are easy to make and are excellent for a number of ailments, including detoxification, coughs, colds, flus, or as a strengthening tonic. Sometimes it is just good medicine. It is quick and easy to make and a great way to use up any miscellaneous wild herbs that have been harvested.

BIENNIALS

Many of the plants growing in meadows are biennials. They develop a basal rosette of leaves the first year and in the second year send up a flower stalk, bloom, and go to seed. The seed stalk turns brown and dies back, but not before dispersing its seeds. Once a biennial has been located, start looking around for its basal leaves. The first-year roots of many of the biennials are edible and can be dug throughout the winter until the plant starts sending up a flower stalk the next spring. These include evening primrose, thistle, burdock, and yellow dock.

WETLANDS

There is a diversity of edible roots found in the swamps and marshes. Digging down into the mud to retrieve the roots can be a challenge, especially in the fall and winter when the water is cold. Roots include cattails, duck potatoes, and groundnuts.

Nuts

The cooler autumn air brings with it a change in leaf color accompanied by nuts maturing and dropping to the ground. Most nuts are sweet, high in protein, and can be used as a substitute for meat in the diet. They are also rich in unsaturated fats that give them a high caloric value but no bad cholesterol. Nuts commonly found in the eastern United States include hazelnuts, beechnuts, walnuts, hickory, and chestnuts.

Nut-Berry Cookies
A sweet and nutty taste of the wild.

- ½ cup butter
- 1 cup cane sugar
- ½ teaspoon vanilla extract
- 2 eggs
- 1 cup flour
- 2 cups oats
- ¼ cup black walnuts, chopped
- ¼ cup dried wild blueberries, rehydrated

Cream together the butter and sugar. Stir in vanilla. Add eggs one at a time, mixing well. Stir in flour and oats, then black walnuts and blueberries. Drop by teaspoonfuls onto a well-greased baking sheet. Bake at 350°F for 10 to 12 minutes.

References

Duke, J. A. (1997). *The green pharmacy.* Emmaus, PA: Rodale Press.

Mindell, E. (1994). *Food as medicine.* New York, NY: Simon & Schuster.

CHAPTER TEN

WILD HERBAL SEASONINGS AND SPICES

Tastes	52
Energetics	53
References	54

Seasonings and spices are plant-derived substances that add flavor and zest to any dish and should be used to enhance, not dominate, the natural flavors of foods. However, spices do more than just add flavor to a dish. Herbs and spices provide necessary nutrients and health benefits to the diet. They can be used to strengthen the body's resistance to disease or as a remedy for common ailments, including digestion, circulation, or for pain and inflammation.

Seasonings and spices come from the leaves, seeds, roots, bark, stems, flowers, or fruits of wild and cultivated herbs. Most spices today are imported, although some are cultivated and grown in the United States. However, there are a number of native and naturalized plants that grow wild that can be harvested and used to add flavor to foods, turning a plain and simple dish into a tasty, gourmet meal.

Tastes

"The energy is in the taste."

—Jim Duke

Plants contain a vast array of phytochemicals. Each herb contains about five thousand biological chemicals, all of which are biologically active. Our genes pull out the ones it needs and discards the rest (Redwood, 2010). Some are nutritional or promote good health while others are potentially toxic. Our sense of taste allows us to recognize and deal with chemicals in plants. Plant defenses that include proteinase inhibitors and lectins are potentially toxic and are not detected by taste but can be destroyed by cooking (Johns, 1996).

TASTING HERBS

Tastes are an indicator of the properties of plants. Tasting plants is one way of getting to know the plant. You can identify it, watch it bloom, and even grow it. But it's not until you taste the plant that you really get to know it. Taste is stimulating to the nervous system and awakens the mind and senses (Frawley and Lad, 1986). It is a mixture of flavors and is an indicator of the properties of plants with different effects for each taste. In Chinese medicine there are five recognized tastes that include sweet, sour, salty, bitter, and pungent (Bone and Mills, 2013). According to Ayurveda, there are six recognized tastes that include sweet, sour, salty, pungent, bitter, and astringent (Frawley and Lad, 1986).

TASTE TEST

When tasting a plant for the first time, try just a little bit. Bite into it, roll it around on your tongue to see which taste buds are activated, and see how it feels. Saliva and mucus in the mouth dissolve the food so it can be tasted. The tongue must be wet to recognize taste. When tasting food that is dry, at first there is no flavor. Holding it in the mouth and moistening it with saliva will eventually bring out the flavors (Silverthorn, 2013).

But sometimes, especially when tasting a wild plant, you detect a taste that just doesn't fit the defined tastes. David Winston has broken it down into ten flavors. These include sweet, salty, mineral salt taste, pungent, cold pungent, spicy, acrid, sour, astringent, and bitter (Winston, 2004). Sometimes, it just tastes "green," like chickweed. Other plants are just bland with no taste. Bland is not generally recognized as a taste. Its only effect is to act as a diuretic (Bone and Mills, 2013). And then there is umami, a taste that is sometimes associated with earthy.

TASTE BUDS

There are four taste buds clustered together on the surface of the tongue that are linked to the tastes of salty, sweet, sour, and bitter. The smell produces the sensation of flavor (Wood, 2009).

Salty

Salt is heating and has a moistening and softening effect. It is alkalizing to the body and moves fluid into the tissues. Sodium is one of the major elements in salt. Salty herbs are high in vitamins and nutrients and enhance the flavor of food, giving it a more earthy quality. It moves fluid and is a diuretic, cleansing the body of toxins. It can also be used to counteract poisoning from poor quality foods. Salt strengthens the digestive system and contributes to the secretion of hydrochloric acid in the stomach (Pitchford, 2002). Without salt, many foods just taste bland.

Salt marsh plants: Plants that grow in a coastal environment with exposure to salt air and brackish water are sources for salt in the wild. These plants have adapted in various ways for survival. For some plants the salt is diluted with water and stored in the stems or leaves, and these include saltwort (*Salicornia* spp.) and sea-beach orach (*Atriplex* spp.). Saltmarsh cordgrass (*Spartina* spp.) excretes salt to the surface of the leaves and can be collected by rubbing the leaf blade between your fingers.

Herbs with salt: There are other herbs that don't grow near the coast that have salt. These include seaweed, violets, chickweed, cleavers, bacopa, self-heal, and nettles.

Sweet

Sweet is the flavor found in most fruits and is a source of vitamins, minerals, and antioxidants that help restore our cells. It is cooling and moistening, helping to relieve thirst, and has a grounding effect. Sweet is sometimes used to reduce the bitter or otherwise unpleasant taste of other herbs. Herbs that contain sugars, starches, or mucilage produce a sweet taste (Frawley and Lad, 1986).

Sour

Sour is derived from a variety of acids, the most common being citric acid, tannic acid, ascorbic acid, and malic acid. Sour is the taste of fruit acids, vinegar, and tannins in cooling herbs. They build strength and reduce inflammation. Sour tastes include leaves of wood sorrel, sheep sorrel, and yellow dock. The sourwood tree is aptly named for the taste of its leaves. Members of the rose family often have sour fruits and include hawthorn, rose hips, plums, and wild cherry. The fruits of sumac and black gum are also sour. Many sour herbs are also astringent and have a drying effect.

Bitter

Bitter is a taste that many people tend to avoid and one that modern agriculture, through selective breeding, is making less bitter and tastier. This also reduces their medicinal value. As Jim Duke often says, "Go to the wild herbs. They haven't been tampered with." These wild herbs can be found in most backyards or gardens and include dandelion, cresses, and yellow dock. Plants produce bitter compounds as a response to predation to avoid being eaten by animals and is often an indicator of toxicity, but a little bitterness can be good. Bitter can accent sweet or moderately sour herbs. Bitter compounds include

oils, tannins, alkaloids, phenols, and flavonoids (Wood, 2009).

The bitter taste stimulates salivary secretions that jump-start the digestive system to secrete enzymes that help digest proteins and stimulates the production of bile, which is needed to help digest fats. If the digestive system is sluggish, use bitters. Using bitters on a regular basis can help prevent heartburn, indigestion, and other digestive issues.

Pungent: Members of the mustard family are pungent or spicy and have a heating effect. When you bite into the leaf of a member of the mustard family, you feel heat. Mustard leaves and seeds are both sources for spicy and pungent flavors. Pungent herbs contain essential oils produced by the plant to protect it from predators and insects. These essential oils are antimicrobial and kill off pathogens. Therapeutic doses can promote sweating, helping to break a fever. They can also help to cool the body during the summer through sweating (Wood, 2009).

Astringent: Astringent is drying and dries up secretions. Tannin is a compound that is astringent and can be found in a number of plants including oaks. An extreme example of astringent is biting into an unripe persimmon.

Energetics

Energetics refer to the patterns of energy, not just in plants but also in people. Tasting herbs is one way to understand the energetics of plants and the framework for choosing which herbs to use in a particular situation. Different tastes have different effects and can be either heating or cooling and drying or moistening. According to Ayurveda, sweet, sour, and salty are moistening and pungent, bitter, and astringent are drying (Frawley and Lad, 1986). Just like plants, people also have these qualities with a unique blend of hot, cold, dry, or moist, referred to as their constitution. Because of this uniqueness, what works for one person may not work for another. It's important to match the herb to the person or the situation.

HEATING HERBS

Some herbs are warming, and you feel the heat when you bite into them. Herbs that are aromatic and spicy are generally warming and stimulating

(Wood, 2009). Pungent, sour, and salty plants are considered heating. Heating herbs are also drying and are beneficial for those who feel cold, damp, or sluggish (de la Forêt, 2017).

COOLING HERBS
Bitter, sweet, and astringent herbs are cooling. Many cooling remedies come from fruits in the rose family. Flowers and fruits of members of this family are rich in flavonoids, the compound that contributes to color. Flavonoids are antioxidants and capillary healers and are cooling. Some flavonoids produce cyanide as they break down. In small doses cyanide can be cooling. These compounds can be detected by the bitter almond smell in members of the rose family, including wild cherry (Wood, 2009). Limonene is an aromatic found in citrus oils that is cooling and tastes sour even though most aromatic herbs are considered pungent and warming (Wood, 2009). Limonene contains antiviral properties in low concentrations. They are used as tonics for the mucous membranes and as nasal decongestants (Pengelly, 2004). Lemon balm, lemon verbena, and lemon thyme are cultivated herbs that contain limonene with a strong citrus scent. Bitter herbs are cooling and drying and have a grounding effect.

MOISTENING HERBS
Sweet, salty, and sour herbs are considered moistening. Demulcent herbs that contain mucilage are moistening to the mucous membranes. When combined with water they have a slimy effect. These herbs are generally cooling and taste either sweet or bland (Pengelly, 2004). Mucilage is not limited to a specific plant part. They may occur in the roots, leaves, bark, or seeds of various plants. The roots of the mallow family are mucilaginous and can be used to make a tea for respiratory or digestive ailments. The bark of slippery elm is mucilaginous and can be dried and ground into a tea as well. Leaves of sassafras are slimy and often used as a thickener in soups.

DRYING HERBS
Astringents are drying and cause tissue to contract. Bitter, pungent, and astringent are drying tastes with pungent as the most astringent (Frawley and Lad, 1986). Herbs that contain tannins are astringent. When tasted, they leave a puckering, drying sensation in the mouth (Pengelly, 2004).

References
Bone, K. A. and Mills, S. (2013). Principles and practice of phytotherapy. New York, NY: Elsevier.

de la Foret, R. (2017). Alchemy of herbs: Transform everyday ingredients into foods & remedies that heal. Carlsbad, CA: Hay House, Inc.

Frawley, D. and Lad, V. (1986). The yoga of herbs: An Ayurvedic guide to herbal medicine. Twin Lakes, WI: Lotus Press.

Pengelly, A. (2004). The constituents of medicinal plants. Cambridge, MA: CABI Publishing.

Pitchford, P. (2002). Healing with whole foods. Berkeley, CA: North Atlantic Books.

Redwood, D. (2010). "Herbal medicine: The healing power of plants." Interview with Jim Duke. Retrieved from http://www.healthyupdate.net/Health/Interview/The_Healing_Power_of_Plants_Interview_with_James_Duke_PhD/310/1.

Silverthorn, D. U. (2013). Human physiology. Boston, MA: Pearson.

Winston, D. (2004). "Herbal energetics." Southwest Conference of Botanical Medicine. Retrieved from https://www.botanical-medicine.org/Herbal-Energetics.

Wood, M. (2009). The earthwise herbal: A complete guide to new world medicinal plants. Berkeley, CA: North Atlantic Books.

CHAPTER ELEVEN

HERBAL TEAS

Infusions and Decoctions   56

Tea Blending and Formulation   56

Teas for Common Ailments   57

Digestion   58

Kidney and Bladder Health   58

Heart Health   59

References   59

One of the easiest ways to introduce wild plants into your diet is in the form of herbal teas. A cup of hot tea first thing in the morning is a great way to start the day. All you need is water and plant material, either fresh or dried. Teas can be made to drink for pure pleasure or to share with friends. They can be served at gatherings, or they can be used to support the body's natural resistance or healing process of a particular ailment. The act of blending and making your own teas can be healing, and even more so when you are able to gather your own plant materials.

Plants contain phytochemicals that are extracted from the plant using water as the solvent, either hot or cold. Solubility is important in tea-making. Solvents are needed to dissolve or extract soluble components from the plant. Water at its boiling point will extract most of the active constituents from an herb (Engels, 2014). The plant material remaining after the soluble components have been extracted is referred to as the marc. The menstruum is the solvent used in the extraction process. True tea technically refers to brews made from the plant *Camellia sinensis* and herbal infusions are referred to as tisanes.

Infusions and Decoctions

Tea-making involves infusing or decocting an herb in water. Infusions involve steeping fresh or dried leaves, flowers, or flowering tops in hot or cold water. Whether to do an infusion or decoction depends on what part of the plant is being used. Soft or delicate parts that include leaves, flowers, and aromatic parts are better as an infusion. Hard parts that include bark, roots, or seeds are better as a decoction and often require a slow simmer to extract the constituents.

COLD INFUSIONS

Cold infusions take longer than hot water infusions, often several hours. Cold infusions are good for plants with constituents that include sugars, proteins, gums, mucilage, pectin, tannins, and essential oils (Green, 2000). A cold infusion, sometimes referred to as a gentle infusion, is prepared at least twelve to twenty-four hours prior to serving. They take longer but are often preferred for some plants, especially aromatic herbs or flower teas. A cold infusion retains volatile oils that are lost with heat.

SOLAR INFUSIONS

Solar infusions are made by placing herbs in a glass jar with water. Set the jar directly in the sunlight for several hours. Be prepared to move the jar as the sun journeys across the sky. Flowers and aromatic herbs are good to use in a solar infusion.

HOT INFUSIONS

Hot infusions are made by pouring boiling or hot water over an herb and letting it steep. The longer it steeps, the stronger the flavor and effects. Length of steeping time varies, depending on how strong you want your tea to be, generally five to ten minutes. For a medicinal tea, steep the tea for ten to thirty minutes or longer.

DECOCTIONS

Decoctions are made with hard plant parts, including bark, roots, thick leaves, and seeds. Start by covering the plant parts with cold water, bringing to a gentle boil, then simmering for twenty to thirty minutes. Turn the heat off, cover the pot, and let it continue to steep for another ten to fifteen minutes for a stronger tea. Harder plant parts require a longer steep time. The ratio of water to herb varies, depending on how strong you want your tea. As a general rule, use 1 tablespoon dried herb per 1 cup water. Teas have a limited shelf life. They may last two to three days in a refrigerator. Alcohol, glycerin, and vinegar can be used as a preservative to extend the shelf life.

Tea Blending and Formulation

Every herb has its own unique flavor and quality. People choose to drink tea because they enjoy the flavor. Knowing what each herb tastes like is important in making tea blends. Blending these flavors and qualities allows you to create your own tea blend based on your personal needs and preferences. Understanding the energetics of the plant and its actions can help you decide which herbs to use for a particular effect or person.

DETERMINE THE DESIRED EFFECT

Blending herbs is basically a four-part process. A primary plant provides the effect you want and should comprise 30 percent to 60 percent of the blend. A secondary plant should have a similar effect and support and enhance the primary plant. It should make up 25 percent to 50 percent of the blend. A tertiary herb is more for flavor and color to make the tea more pleasant and should make up 10 percent to 25 percent of the formula. A quaternary herb acts as a conductor and brings it all together. Pick an herb that improves absorption. This would include plants that are rich in terpenes, flavonoids, and saponins and should only be 10 percent to 15 percent of the blend (Spellman, 2012).

SYNERGY

Blending herbs with similar actions is a great way to combine the synergistic effects of the herbs. Blends can be used as a remedy for a specific ailment or to prevent illnesses from happening. When blending teas, avoid combining roots with leaves or plants that are decocted with plants that are infused. The two can be made separately and then combined.

Sleep-eze Tea Blend
Relax, restore, refresh.

- 13 grams lemon balm (*Melissa officinalis*)
- 7 grams passionflower (*Passiflora incarnate*)
- 7 grams chamomile (*Matricaria chamomilla*)
- 5 grams oat straw (*Avena sativa*)
- 4 grams skullcap (*Scutellaria lateriflora*)

Mix dried herbs in a large bowl. Store in a closed container in dark pantry.

To make a cup of tea:
Add 4 grams mixed herbs to a cup or teapot. Add 1 cup hot water, cover, and let steep for 10 to 15 minutes. Strain.

Teas for Common Ailments

Knowing which herbs can be used to make a tea for common ailments can empower you to take your health into your own hands. Many common ailments can be treated with teas made from herbs that are growing all around us. When choosing herbs to make tea, think about what effect you want the herbs to have.

STRESS

Stress is a part of life. It is our body's response to challenging situations by sending nerve signals from the brain to several glands. Herbs can be used to support the nervous system by keeping it healthy and preventing illnesses resulting from stress. The act of growing and picking your own herbs or spending time in nature can lower stress as well.

Adaptogens

Adaptogens are herbs that help the body deal with stress. They can help restore balance and increase resistance to emotional, physical, and environmental stressors (Winston and Maimes, 2007) and are easy to brew into a tea.

Nervines

Nervines are herbs that support the nervous system. Nervine tonics strengthen and restore nerve tissues damaged from shock and stress (Hoffman, 2003). These tonics are generally high in calcium, magnesium, B vitamins, and protein (Gladstar, 2008). Nerve tonic herbs include oats, skullcap, St. John's wort, hops, chamomile, and lemon balm.

Nervine sedatives help relax the nervous system and reduce tension and pain. There are a number of herbs that have sedative effects. Which herb to use is often determined by what's growing around you. Included among the nervine sedatives are skullcap, passionvine, motherwort, linden, lemon balm, wild lettuce, hops, and St. John's wort.

Herbs can be used to gently nourish and stimulate the system by increasing circulation, providing nutrients, and increasing vitality (Gladstar, 2008). Known as nervine stimulants, herbs such as prickly ash and wax myrtle activate the nervous system.

Stress Relief
Drink this calming and relaxing tea at night before going to bed to promote a restful sleep.

- ½ cup linden flowers
- 1 teaspoon skullcap leaves or flowers
- 1 teaspoon passionvine leaves
- ½ teaspoon St. John's wort flowers
- 1 teaspoon life everlasting leaves and flowers
- 1 teaspoon lemon balm leaves
- Simple syrup to taste (recipe below)

Blend herbs and add hot water to 1 tablespoon herb mix. Let sit for 10 to 15 minutes. Strain and drink. Sweeten with simple syrup if desired.

Simple Syrup
Use as a sweetener in herb teas or other beverages.

- 1 cup water
- 1 cup organic cane sugar

Put water and sugar in saucepan and bring to a gentle boil. Reduce heat and cook another 5 minutes. Cool and use as a sweetener.

Digestion
Carminative herbs can be used to soothe an upset stomach or gastrointestinal distress. Peppermint and chamomile are carminatives that can help soothe the digestive system. Digestive bitters sipped before you eat as an aperitif or after your meal as a digestif can help prevent and treat heartburn and acid reflux. The bitter taste provides what is often lacking in our diet. Dandelion root is a popular primary herb used in formulating bitters.

Dandelion Bitters
Drink as an aperitif before dinner to stimulate the digestive system.

- 4–5 dandelion roots and leaves, chopped
- 1 yellow dock root, chopped
- ¼ cup orange peel
- 4–6 cardamom pods
- 1 quart vodka
- 3–5 sprigs peppermint

Cover herbs with vodka. Store in a dark pantry for 6 to 8 weeks.

Digest-Ade
Soothe the tummy with this herbal blend for indigestion or gastrointestinal discomfort.

- 1 tablespoon peppermint
- 1 teaspoon chamomile
- 1 teaspoon mallow root
- 1 teaspoon dandelion leaves

Add two cups hot water. Cover and steep for 10 to 15 minutes. Strain and drink.

Kidney and Bladder Health
Diuretics and laxatives can help with kidney and bladder discomfort. Cranberries (*Vaccinium macrocarpon*), blueberries (*Vaccinium* spp.), and stonebreak (*Phyllanthus niruri*) are all herbs that help with urinary problems.

Stone Break Tea
Promotes healthy kidneys and bladder.

- 2 teaspoons cornsilk (*Zea mays*)
- 2 teaspoons bearberry (*Arctostaphylos uva-ursi*)
- 3 teaspoons cranberry/blueberry/bilberry (*Vaccinium* spp.)
- 2 teaspoons stinging nettles (*Urtica dioica*)
- 1 teaspoon chanca piedra (*Phyllanthus niruri*)
- 1 teaspoon plantain leaves (*Plantago* spp.)

Blend herbs together. Use 1 tablespoon per 1 cup hot water. Cover and let steep for 10 to 15 minutes. Strain and drink as needed.

Heart Health

The heart is the workhorse of the body. It is the powerhouse of the circulatory system. Herbs that stimulate the circulatory system include prickly ash (*Zanthoxylum* spp.) and wax myrtle (*Morella cerifera*).

Hypertension refers to elevated blood pressure. Stress and anxiety cause spikes in blood pressure so calming, relaxing herbs are good to use to reduce stress. They include passionvine (*Passiflora incarnata*), skullcap (*Scutellaria lateriflora*), linden (*Tilia americana*), and St. John's wort (*Hypericum punctatum*). Hawthorn (*Crataegus* spp.) berries, leaves, and flowers also serve as a mild antihypertensive and relaxant (peripheral dilator), easing contraction while dilating the vessels for improved circulation. Combine linden (*Tilia americana*) flowers with hawthorn for the treatment of nervousness and mild hypertension.

Heart Healthy Tea

- 2 teaspoons hawthorn powder
- 1 teaspoon hibiscus flowers
- 3 teaspoons linden flowers
- 1 teaspoon rose petals

Pour hot water over herbs, cover, and steep for 10 to 15 minutes.

Herbal Tea Blends

Suggested use: 1 tablespoon herb blend infused in 1 cup hot water for 10 to 15 minutes. Strain and drink.

The following suggested blends are herbs that grow wild or can be easily cultivated. These blends can be adapted to taste preferences or availability of herbs. The quantity listed is for dried herbs and will make four cups. When using fresh herbs, triple the amount.

Fever-Redux

This herb blend will promote sweating and help to break a fever.

- 1 tablespoon feverfew leaves and flowers
- 1 teaspoon yarrow leaves
- 1 tablespoon peppermint leaves and flowers
- 1 teaspoon elderflowers
- 1 teaspoon boneset leaves and flowers

Stomach Relief

For diarrhea or irritable bowels, try this astringent and soothing tea.

- 1 tablespoon yarrow leaves
- 1 teaspoon peppermint leaves
- 1 teaspoon wax myrtle leaves
- 1 teaspoon chamomile flowers
- 1 tablespoon plantain leaves

References

Engels, G. *ABC's of Herbal Extractions*. Retrieved from https://www.youtube.com/watch?v=W1WeKS7NsSM

Gladstar, R. (2008). *Rosemary Gladstar's herbal recipes for vibrant health*. North Adams, MA: Storey Publishing.

Green, J. 2000. *The herbal medicine-maker's handbook: A home manual*. New York, NY: Crossing Press.

Hoffman, D. (2003). *Medical herbalism: The science and practice of herbal medicine*. Rochester, VT: Healing Arts Press.

Spellman, K. (2012). Lecture Notes, "Fundamentals of Herbal Medicine." Tai Sophia University.

Winston, D. and Maimes, S. (2007). *Adaptogens: Herbs for strength, stamina, and stress relief*. Rochester, VT: Healing Arts Press.

CHAPTER TWELVE

HERBAL VINEGARS AND SYRUPS

Shrubs   62

Oxymels   62

Syrups   62

References   63

Shrubs

Vinegar is warming but it can taste sour or bitter so adding honey or fruit to an herbal vinegar can help reduce sourness or bitterness. Shrubs are drinks made from fruit, vinegar, and honey. They can be drunk alone or added to hot or cold water. Sparkling water adds a little fizz to the drink.

Blackberry Shrub

Add ice and drink on a hot summer day.

- 2 cups fresh blackberries
- 1 cup organic cane sugar
- ¼ cup water
- 2 cups organic balsamic vinegar
- 2 cups sparkling water (optional)

Place blackberries, sugar, and water in a saucepan and bring to a boil. Continue to boil for about 10 minutes. Cool. Add vinegar, cover, and let sit for at least two weeks. Drink as is or add sparkling water for a bubbly drink.

Wild Strawberry Shrub

A delightful berry flavor of spring.

- 2 cups wild strawberries
- 1 cup rice vinegar
- ½ cup honey

Combine all ingredients in a quart jar. Cover and let sit for at least two weeks. Strain and serve with sparkling water.

Oxymels

Oxymels are a mixture of herbs with both honey and vinegar, usually two parts vinegar to one part honey. You can use fresh or dried herbs (Boardwine, 2020).

Beebalm Oxymel

- 1 pint fresh beebalm (*Monarda didyma*) leaves and flowers, chopped
- ½ cup honey
- Organic apple cider vinegar

Fill a mason jar with chopped herbs. Add the honey and cover with vinegar, leaving an inch or two of space at the top. Cover and let sit for 2 to 4 weeks, shaking frequently. Strain and use as a salad dressing or as a marinade on vegetables.

Syrups

Herbal medicine can make a sick person feel better but the taste is often so unpleasant that they don't take it. Syrups were traditionally administered as better-tasting medicine for both children and adults. Even the best medicine will more likely be taken if it tastes good.

Linden Flower Syrup

A mild-tasting syrup to use as a sweetener or add to sparkling water.

- 4 cups linden flowers
- 5 cups water
- 1 cup sugar

Place linden flowers in a quart jar. In a separate pot, combine water and sugar and heat to boiling. Lower heat and continue to cook for 5 more minutes to make a syrup. Pour syrup over linden flowers. Cover and store in the refrigerator and use as a sweetener.

Black Cherry Syrup

A great sweetener to add to your favorite tea or beverage.

- 2 cups black cherry juice
- 1 cup organic cane sugar

Combine juice and sugar in a saucepan and bring to a boil. Continue to cook for 25 to 30 minutes, stirring frequently. Pour into sterilized jars and seal.

References

Boardwine, T. (2020). "Oxymels: Vinegar as menstruum." Medicines from the Earth symposium notes.

CHAPTER THIRTEEN

TINCTURES, CORDIALS, AND ELIXIRS

Tinctures   66

Cordials   66

Elixirs   67

Tinctures

Tinctures are extracts of plants and are typically combined with alcohol, glycerin, or vinegar as the preservative. Alcohol extracts more types of constituents than any other solvent except water and has a longer shelf life than vinegar. Glycerites taste sweet and are easily diluted in water. It has half the solvent power of ethyl alcohol, so more plant material is needed. For fresh herbs, use 80 percent glycerin and 20 percent water. Dried herbs should contain 60 percent to 70 percent glycerin and 30 percent to 40 percent water. Avoid resinous or oily herbs. Herbs preserved with glycerin have a shorter shelf life than those with alcohol.

SOLUBILITY

It's important to know what solvent works best for different herbs. Most constituents can be extracted with hot water. Some herbs are water soluble, not alcohol soluble. These include tannins and mucilage. Other herbs, like usnea, need heat and alcohol.

The folk method is what many people use, especially in the beginning. This involves placing the herb in a jar, covering it with alcohol, letting it steep for a period of time, then straining it. This is fine for family and friends.

The apothecary method involves weighing and measuring everything and keeping a record of these measurements. You would typically use this process if you wanted to market your product or use it in a clinical setting.

Cordials

Cordials are extracts from fruits or herbs and are a great way to make better-tasting medicine. They are meant to warm, stimulate, and aid digestion. To make a cordial, begin with a tincture of an herb or fruit infused in alcohol and add a sweetener if desired. Cordials can be added to tea, juice, and any other drink or can be drunk as is.

Wild Blueberry Cordial

- 2 cups fresh wild blueberries
- 1 cup organic cane sugar
- ¼ cup water
- 2 cups alcohol (vodka, brandy, whiskey)
- 1 vanilla bean, halved lengthwise, optional

Bring berries, sugar, and water to a gentle boil. Lower heat and continue to cook for about 10 minutes. Cool. Add alcohol and vanilla bean if desired. Cover and store in a dark pantry for at least two weeks or until ready to use.

Black Cherry Cordial

A blood builder and strengthener for that hot summer day.

- 1 cup black cherry juice
- ¼ cup maple syrup
- ¼ cup crème de cacao
- 1 vanilla bean, halved lengthwise
- ¾ cup vodka

Combine ingredients. Let steep for two weeks. Serve over ice.

Elixirs

Elixirs are made with tonic herbs, spices, and fruits. They provide nourishment and balance body systems and organs.

Dandelion Flower Elixir

A strengthener to drink as is or added to your favorite beverage.

- 1 cup dandelion flowers, separated from the base
- 1 cup vodka
- ½ cup orange liqueur
- ½ cup lemon liqueur
- ½ orange, sliced
- ½ lemon, sliced

Combine ingredients. Cover and store in a dark pantry for at least two weeks.

Heartwarming Elixir

A strengthener for the heart.

- ½ cup fresh rose hips
- ½ cup dried hawthorn berries
- ¾ cup organic ginger, sliced
- 1½ cups honey
- 2 inches cinnamon stick
- 1¼ cups apple jack brandy

Cut ends off rose hips and cut in half. Place in saucepan with hawthorns and cover with water. Bring water to a gentle boil, reduce heat, and simmer until the liquid is reduced by half. Let cool. Place sliced ginger in a mason jar, then add honey and cinnamon stick. Strain cooled tea into ginger mixture. Add brandy. Cover and store in dark closet.

CHAPTER FOURTEEN

HERB-INFUSED OILS

Oil Infusions   70

Salves   70

Lotions   70

References   70

Oil Infusions

Oil can be used as a menstruum to infuse herbs for medicinal and culinary purposes. Fixed or carrier oils are often used for herbal infusions because they don't evaporate when exposed to air. Volatile oils include essential and aromatic oils that evaporate readily when exposed to air (Green, 2000). Herbal oil infusions used on the skin provide a protective covering and facilitate the absorption of herbal constituents. Herbs can be either fresh or dried when added to an oil infusion.

HERB OIL

For fresh herb oil, allow fresh herbs to wilt for twelve to twenty-four hours to reduce the moisture in the leaves. Chop or grind plant material to a fine pulp. Add a fixed oil of your choice (olive, sweet almond, grapeseed, coconut) to cover the herbs. Let sit for 2 weeks.

For dried herb oil, grind the dried herb to a powder. Add a fixed oil of your choice.

When your infusion is complete, strain the oil from the herb using a tincture press or strainer lined with muslin. Let sit for a few days until the sediment settles at the bottom. Decant and filter for use.

Salves

Herbal oils are the primary ingredient for making salves and lotions for topical use, or sometimes in the ears. Salves are an oil extract mixed with a thickener/stabilizer, often beeswax, to allow them to be spread on the skin.

Basic Salve

- 1 cup herb oil infusion
- 1 ounce grated beeswax

Warm the oil infusion and beeswax over low heat until the wax is fully melted. Pour into containers and let cool.

Lotions

Lotions are a blend of oil in water. An emulsifying agent such as beeswax and lecithin is often necessary to suspend the oil in the water.

Herbal Lotion

- 5 ounces distilled water
- 2½ ounces aloe vera gel
- 2½ ounces jojoba oil
- 1 tablespoon shea butter
- ½ ounce beeswax, grated
- 6 ounces herbal oil infusion
- 10 drops lemongrass essential oil
- 10 drops vitamin E
- 16 (1-ounce) containers

Let distilled water and aloe vera gel sit until they are at room temperature, then mix together and set aside. Combine the remaining ingredients in a glass cooking pan and heat over low heat until the beeswax has melted. Pour into a blender and cool to room temperature. While mixture is cooling, get the containers ready. Once cooled, turn the blender on high speed and slowly pour in the water and aloe vera gel mixture. Pour the herbal lotion into containers and allow to cool.

References

Green, J. 2000. *The herbal medicine-maker's handbook: A home manual.* New York, NY: Crossing Press.

PART 4
MEET THE HERBS

Bacopa (*Bacopa monnieri*)   74

Beautyberry (*Callicarpa americana*)   75

Beebalm (*Monarda didyma*)   76

Black Gum (*Nyssa sylvatica*)   77

Black Haw (*Viburnum prunifolium*)   79

Black Walnut (*Juglans nigra*)   80

Black Willow (*Salix nigra*)   81

Blackberries, Raspberries, and Dewberries
(*Rubus* spp.)   82

Blueberries and Huckleberries
(*Vaccinium* spp., *Gaylussacia* spp.)   84

Bugleweed (*Lycopus virginica, L. americana*)   85

Burdock (*Arctium minus, A. lappa*)   86

Cattails (*Typha latifolia, T. angustifolia*)   87

Chickweed (*Stellaria media*)   88

Cleavers (*Galium aparine*)   89

Corn Salad (*Valerianella radiata, V. locusta*)   90

Crabapple (*Malus* spp.)   91

Dandelion (*Taraxacum officinale*)   92

Elder (*Sambucus canadensis*)   94

Evening Primrose (*Oenothera biennis*)   96

Field Garlic (*Allium vineale, Allium* spp.)   97

Goldenrod (*Solidago* spp.)   98

Ground Cherry (*Physalis* spp.)   99

Groundnuts (*Apios americana*)   100

Hazelnut (*Corylus americana*)   101

Hickory (*Carya* spp.)   102

Horsemint (*Monarda punctata*)   103

Indian Pipe (*Monotropa uniflora*)   104

Linden (*Tilia americana*)   105

Mallow (*Hibiscus* spp.)   106

Mulberry (*Morus rubra, M. alba*)   108

Mullein (*Verbascum thapsus*)   109

Nettles (*Urtica dioica, Laportea canadensis*)   111

Oaks (*Quercus* spp.)   113

Passionvine (*Passiflora incarnata*)   115

Pawpaw (*Asimina triloba*)   116

Persimmon (*Diospyrus virginiana*)   118

Pine (*Pinus* spp.)   119

Plantain (*Plantago major, P. lanceolata*)   121

Plum (*Prunus* spp.)   122

Poke (*Phytolacca americana*)   123

Prickly Ash
(*Zanthoxylum americanum, Z. clava-herculis*)   124

Purslane (*Portulaca oleracea*)   125

Red Clover (*Trifolium pretense*)   126

Redbud (*Cercis canadensis*)   127

Sassafras (*Sassafras albidum*)   128

Self-Heal, Heal-All (*Prunella vulgaris*)   130

Serviceberry (*Amelanchier* spp.)   131

Skullcap (*Scutellaria lateriflora*)   132

Sorrel (*Rumex acetosella, Oxalis* spp.)   133

Spicebush (*Lindera benzoin*)   134

St. John's wort (*Hypericum punctatum*)   135

Sumac (*Rhus* spp.)   136

Thistles (*Cirsium* spp.)   138

Usnea Lichen (*Usnea* spp.)   139

Violet (*Viola* spp.)   141

Wax myrtle (*Morella cerifera*)   142

Wild Beans (*Strophostyles helvola, S. umbellata*)   143

Wild Black Cherry (*Prunus serotina*)   144

Wild Grapes (*Vitis* spp.)   146

Wild Lettuce (*Lactuca canadensis*)   148

Wild Mustard (*Alliaria petiolata, Barbarea* spp., *Brassica* spp., *Capsella bursa-pastoris, Cardamine* spp., *Lepidium virginicum*)   149

Wild Rose (*Rosa* spp.)   152

Yarrow (*Achillea millefolium*)   153

Yaupon (*Ilex vomitoria*)   154

Yellow Dock (*Rumex crispus*)   155

Yucca (*Yucca filamentosa, Y. aloifolia*)   156

BACOPA
(Bacopa monnieri)
Plantain Family (Plantaginaceae)

Description
Bacopa is a plant that is native to India, sometimes called brahmi, and has been known and used for improving memory, epilepsy, and as a mild sedative (Sahelian, 2019). It is native to the United States and can be found along the east coast from Virginia south into Florida along drainage ditches, muddy banks, and marshes. Also known as water hyssop, bacopa is a succulent perennial that forms mats across wetlands. It is a low-growing, succulent plant with smooth, shiny leaves that are paired and rounded at the tops. Solitary flowers arise from the nodes and are white to pinkish in color with five petals.

Part Used
Aerial parts

Preparation and Uses
Bacopa can be eaten fresh and added to salads or it can be dried and made into a tea by steeping the dried herb in hot water. It can also be tinctured in alcohol and taken as needed.

Brain Booster
A stimulating tincture for a mental and physical energy boost.

- 15 milliliters bacopa (*Bacopa monnieri*)
- 10 milliliters ginseng (*Eleutherococcus senticosus*)
- 5 milliliters prickly ash (*Zanthoxylum* spp.)

Combine herbs and add to a 1-ounce tincture bottle. Take one dropper when needed for that extra boost of mental or physical energy.

Nutritional and Medicinal Benefits
Bacopa is a mental stimulant as well as a nervine tonic, mild anticonvulsive, antispasmodic, and antioxidant (Winston and Maimes, 2007). It is a bitter herb that has a salty taste, especially if it's growing near the ocean. Bacopa is rich in potassium.

Chemical Constituents
Bacopa constituents include alkaloids brahmine and herpestine, glycosides, and saponins (Kuhn and Winston, 2008).

Growing Bacopa
Bacopa grows naturally in marshes and wet, boggy areas. A shallow pool works great for growing bacopa.

Safety Precautions
Water quality is important when harvesting bacopa from wet areas. Bacopa absorbs whatever chemicals are in the water and should therefore be harvested from organic sources or clean water.

References
Kuhn, M. A., and Winston, D. (2008). *Herbal therapy & supplements: A scientific and traditional approach*. Philadelphia, PA: Wolters Kluwer/Lippincott Williams & Wilkins.

Sahelian, R. (2019). "Benefit and side effects, safety, research studies, dosage interactions with other supplements and medications." Retrieved from https://www.raysahelian.com/bacopa.html.

Winston, D. and Maimes, S. (2007). *Adaptogens: Herbs for strength, stamina, and stress relief*. Rochester, VT: Healing Arts Press.

BEAUTYBERRY
(Callicarpa americana)
Mint Family (Lamiaceae)

Description
Beautyberry is a deciduous shrub that is native to the southeastern United States and grows from Maryland, west to Tennessee, and south to Florida and Texas. It grows in full sun to part shade, often along the edges of forests in the under-story. It grows up to twelve feet tall with arching branches that bear small, pink flowers in dense clusters at the base of the leaves from early- to mid-summer. Following the flowers are bright, purple fruits that ripen in the fall and remain on the plant into the winter, providing an important food source for many species of birds. The genus name comes from the Greeks and means beautiful fruit.

Preparation and Uses
Beautyberry offers more than just beautiful berries. A traditional folk remedy was known and used by the country people in Mississippi to offer relief from biting insects while on horseback. They would cut the branches with the leaves attached, crush the leaves, then place the branches between the harness and the horse to keep biting flies and mosquitoes away (Pons, 2006).

Chemical Constituents
Beautyberry's reputation as an insect repellent got the attention of the USDA ARS in 2004 and initiated the investigation of the plant's potential use as a natural insect repellent. Scientific research studies over a twelve-month period identified callicarpenal, intermedeol, and spathulenol as naturally occurring chemicals that repel insects.

Growing Conditions
Beautyberry is easy to grow from seed and from transplants. It prefers full to partly shady conditions with well-drained soil.

References
Pons, Luis. (2007). "Learning from our elders: Folk remedy yields mosquito-thwarting compound." *Agriculture Research.* Retrieved from https://agresearchmag.ars.usda.gov/2006/feb/mosquito.

University of Mississippi. "Scientists Confirm Folk Remedy Repels Mosquitoes." *ScienceDaily,* 3 July 2006. www.sciencedaily.com/releases/2006/07/060703091932.htm.

BEEBALM
(*Monarda didyma*)
Mint Family (Lamiaceae)

Description
Like all members of the mint family, beebalm has paired leaves and a square stem. Its aromatic leaves are oval- to lance-shape. A head-like cluster of bright red, tubular flowers, often with colored bracts, top the plant during the summer months.

Harvesting and Preparation
Beebalm should be harvested at the peak of flowering, about two-thirds down the stem. The entire plant can be dried and used for making teas. Its leaves and flowers can be used for making tinctures.

Medicinal Benefits and Energetics
Monarda is a stimulating nervine. The taste is pungent and sweet. It is a diaphoretic and can be used to reduce fevers and to support the bronchials (Wood, 2009). Beebalm can be used as a mouthwash for gum infections.

Chemical Constituents
Members of the genus *Monarda* contain a high content of thymol, a powerful antiseptic for internal and external use (Johnson, 2015).

Growing Conditions
Beebalm likes moist, well-drained soils but will tolerate some shade. It can be started with plants or seeds. Sow seeds after all danger of frost, cover with loose dirt, and keep moist until seedlings emerge.

References
Johnson, J. (2015). "Benefits of bee balm: Monarda fistulosa and M. didyma." Herbal Academy. Retrieved from https://theherbalacademy.com /benefits-of-bee-balm-monarda-fistulosa -and-m-didyma/.

Wood, M. (2009). *The earthwise herbal: A complete guide to new world medicinal plants*. Berkeley, CA: North Atlantic Books.

BLACK GUM
(Nyssa sylvatica)
Dogwood Family (Nyssaceae)

Description

Black gum is a native deciduous tree that is easy to spot in the fall. This is the time of year when the black gum makes its brilliant appearance. It is one of the first trees whose leaves start changing colors. Its oval-shaped leaves are slightly thickened and glossy green with smooth edges. The leaves turn scarlet red, usually in September in the southeast. Leaves cluster together at the ends of branches and are broadest near the tip.

 When you're driving down the road and you see a tree whose leaves are brilliantly red while the leaves of other trees around it are still green, you can be pretty certain it is the black gum tree. Black gum can be found in dry, upland forests and swamp margins. Its range extends from northeastern states, including Maine, all the way to Florida and west to Texas.

Spring is when black gum blooms, producing flowers that are small and greenish. They grow at the ends of long stalks at the base of new leaves in the spring. Male and female flowers are usually on separate trees, although some trees may have mostly male flowers while others have mostly female flowers. The fruits begin to ripen in mid-September, about the time the leaves turn flaming red. They hang in pairs, sometimes in threes, at the end of a long stalk at the base of the leaves. The fruits are small, less than half an inch, and often go unnoticed since they are partially hidden by the leaves. There is a hard stone with ridges in the center with juicy pulp surrounding it. When ripe, they turn a bluish-black color and drop to the ground. The fruits, also known as sour gum, are the parts that are edible. The name sour gum refers to the sharply acidic flavor, kind of like biting into a sour lemon, which makes it so interesting and unique.

N. sylvatica has the smallest fruits, which might be the reason it hasn't gotten a lot of attention in the wild foods realm. The fruits are also well hidden among the leaves. The swamp black gum (*N. biflora*) has fruits that are larger but have a more bitter aftertaste. The swamp black gum is often confused with the black gum but has recently been classified as its own species. Black gum generally grows in upland forests and stream bottoms whereas swamp black gum grows on heavy clay soils of wet bottomlands.

Growing in the swamps is water tupelo (*N. aquatica*), with fruits that are considerably larger but much more bitter. It is often seen growing in pure stands or mixed with bald cypress trees and has a large buttress that helps stabilize it in swampy waters.

The gum most typically used is Ogeechee gum (*N. ogeche*). The fruits are larger than the black gum, up to one-and-a-half inches long, and turn reddish-orange when ripe. Sometimes called Ogeechee limes, they are a popular lime substitute. Its range, though, is limited to the extreme southeast, primarily the Florida wetlands or along streams and low-lying areas.

Parts Used
Ripe fruits

Preparation and Uses
The fruits of the black gum and Ogeechee gum can be nibbled raw but the best way to use them as a food is to extract the juice. Place the berries in a saucepan, cover with just enough water to prevent them from scorching, and bring to a gentle boil. Reduce the heat and continue to cook until the juice runs freely. Once the juice has started flowing, press through a strainer or food mill to separate the juice from the seeds. Juice extracted from the berries can then be used to make jelly, sauces, and syrup or added as flavoring to drinks or pies. The fruits have lots of pectin, so no commercial pectin needs to be added when making jelly.

Black Gum Wraps

A tasty way to enjoy the wild flavor of black gum berries.

- ¼ cup black gum syrup
- 1 (8-ounce) package cream cheese
- Wonton wraps
- Coconut oil

Blend syrup and cream cheese. Place 1 teaspoon of mixture into the center of a wonton wrap. Moisten edges of the wrap and fold. Heat coconut oil in a skillet and brown the wonton wrap on each side. Repeat for remaining wonton wraps.

Taste and Energetics

Black gum fruits taste like a sour lemon and are cooling.

Growing Black Gums

Black gums grow best on moist, well-drained soil. Transplant as a young sapling in the spring or start from seeds after overwintering them. It grows about a foot a year.

References

Deane, G. (n. d.) Tupelos: Black, swamp, bear, water, ogeechee. Eat the Weeds and other things, too. Retrieved from http://www.eattheweeds.com/nyssus-tart-botanical-tangles-2/.

McGee, C. E. & Outcalt, K. W. (n. d.) "Nyssa sylvatica Marsh. Black Tupelo." Retrieved from http://www.na.fs.fed.us/pubs/silvics_manual/volume_2/nyssa/silvatica.htm.

BLACK HAW
(*Viburnum prunifolium*)
Moschatel Family (Adoxaceae)

Description
Black haw is a deciduous understory shrub that grows in moist woods, thickets, and along stream banks across the eastern United States. It reaches heights up to twenty feet with a spreading crown. Black haw blooms in the spring with a white, flat-topped cluster of flowers followed by berry-like fruits that hang in groups. They start out yellowish-green and then turn blue-black as they ripen. The leaves grow in pairs and are elliptic to ovate in shape and finely toothed.

Uses
Black haw is both food and medicine. The fruits are the food, and the bark is the medicine. The berries are sweet and ripen in the fall, sometimes lingering on into the winter. The bark can be harvested in the spring before the leaves have fully emerged. It can then be dried and used in a tea or tincture. The taste is bitter and astringent.

Black Haw Puree
A dark, rich pulp that has a look and texture of chocolate.
Extract the pulp by heating the fruits on medium heat with just enough water so that they don't stick. Cook until the juice is flowing. Pour through a food mill or strainer to remove the seeds.

Black Haw Biscuits
A naturally sweet biscuit served with honey and butter.

- 1 cup biscuit mix
- ⅓ cup cocoa powder
- ⅓ cup butter, softened
- 2 eggs
- ½ cup black haw pulp
- ⅛ teaspoon cardamom

Mix biscuit mix and cocoa powder together and set aside. In a separate bowl, blend butter and eggs. Add in black haw pulp and cardamom. Stir into biscuit and cocoa powder mix. Drop by spoonful on oiled baking sheet. Bake at 350°F for 12 minutes.

Medicinal Benefits
Black haw is used as an antispasmodic for menstrual cramps and other female problems (Kuhn and Winston, 2008). It is also a nervine and used to treat mild to moderate hypertension (Hoffman, 2003).

Constituents
The bark includes coumarins, phenolic acids, biflavones, and triterpenes (Hoffman, 2003).

Growing Black Haw
Black haw can be started from seed, but also does well when transplanted as a young seedling. Black haw does best in partial shade but will produce more flowers and fruits if it gets more sun.

References
Hoffman, D. (2003). *Medical herbalism: The science and practice of herbal medicine*. Rochester, VT: Healing Arts Press.
Kuhn, M. A., and Winston, D. (2008). *Herbal therapy & supplements: A scientific and traditional approach*. Philadelphia, PA: Wolters Kluwer/ Lippincott Williams & Wilkins.

BLACK WALNUT
(Juglans nigra)
Walnut Family (Juglandaceae)

Description

Black walnuts are found in the eastern half of the United States except for the northern border. They are large trees with compound leaves consisting of seven to nineteen toothed leaflets that turn yellow in autumn. The fruit is a thick-shelled nut with ridges enclosed in a green husk that does not split open at maturity.

Harvesting Black Walnuts

Walnuts begin dropping to the ground in mid-September and should be gathered soon after falling. If they remain on the ground for more than a few days, they become infested with maggots and turn black. Wearing gloves is a must when removing the outer hulls (unless you don't mind sporting stained hands for several weeks).

The easiest way to remove the husks is to place walnuts in the driveway and run them over in your car. Break away the hulls and rinse the nuts in a bucket of water, removing any that float. Spread in a single layer on mats to dry. Once dry, they can be stored in a cool, dry place until needed.

The shells of black walnuts are thick and hard with deep ridges. Use a hammer or a hard rock and a concrete block to crack the walnuts. Position the walnut on its side and give it a firm whack. You may have to practice a bit to develop the right technique for removing the nutmeat in large pieces.

Uses

Place the nutmeats in a food chopper or blender for use in cookies or cakes. Due to their high caloric value and strong flavor, they should be used in small quantities.

Blueberry Walnut Scones

- 2 cups biscuit mix
- ¼ cup butter, softened
- ¼ cup maple yogurt
- ½ cup wild blueberries
- ¼ cup chopped black walnuts

Combine all ingredients. Drop by spoonsful on an ungreased baking dish. Bake at 350°F for 12 to 15 minutes.

Nutritional and Medicinal Benefits

Black walnuts have been referred to as brain food due to their high serotonin content. According to Jim Duke, black walnut, which looks like a brain, is the best source of serotonin. This is befitting of the "Doctrine of Signatures" which is based on "like cures like" and that the shape or color of a plant indicates its use. In this case, the brain-shaped nut is the best source of brain food. The green outer hull can be tinctured and used to treat parasites and ringworm.

Caution

Black walnuts produce juglone, a toxic substance that is found in all parts of the black walnut tree, but especially in the buds, hulls, and roots. The toxic effects can be felt from as far as eighty feet away. Many cultivated vegetables are sensitive to juglone and may be stunted, and wilt or die (Joy and Hudelson, 2010).

References

Joy, A. and Hudelson, B. (2010). "Black Walnut Toxicity." Wisconsin Horticulture, Division of Extension. Retrieved from https://hort .extension.wisc.edu/articles/black-walnut-toxicity/.

BLACK WILLOW
(Salix nigra)
Willow Family (Salicaceae)

Description
Black willow is a small tree that is native to eastern North America. It is valued as a buffer tree in wetland areas, stabilizing the banks and preventing shoreline erosion. The long, narrow leaves are finely saw-toothed and slightly curved to one side. There are both male and female trees, with drooping catkins on the male in early spring. The females release their seeds about mid-spring. The seeds are enclosed in a cotton ball that is carried by the wind for distribution.

Part Used
Inner bark

Preparation and Uses
Willow has traditionally been used as an anti-inflammatory and analgesic to reduce fevers, aches and pains, and inflammation. It was also used to wash wounds and poulticed on sore joints and muscle pain (Kuhn and Winston, 2008).

Pain Relief
A blend of analgesic herbs to provide relief from headaches and muscle aches.

- 45 milliliters black willow
- 20 milliliters Indian pipe
- 20 milliliters wild lettuce
- 15 milliliters meadowsweet
- 40 milliliters prickly ash
- 10 milliliters sweet birch

Combine herbs and add to a 1-ounce tincture bottle. Take 1 teaspoon as needed to help relieve pain. Warning: May cause drowsiness.

Chemical Constituents
Willow bark contains salicylic acid, a simple phenol that has antipyretic and anti-inflammatory properties, useful for treating fevers and arthritis (Bone and Mills, 2013). It also contains tannins and flavonoids. Willow twigs contain indolebutyric acid, a hormone that encourages rooting by soaking cuttings in willow water or it can be used with rooted cuttings for stronger roots (Dalziel, 2021).

Preparation
Bark is best stripped from the branches in the early spring, just before the leaves have fully developed. This is when it peels off most easily in long strips. Spread the bark on mats to dry for several days, then cut into small pieces to use in teas. Decoct two parts water to one part bark. Bring to a gentle boil, reduce to low heat, and simmer until the liquid is reduced by half. To make a tincture, prepare the tea as described above, then add an equal amount of grain alcohol to the tea with the bark included. Let steep for at least two weeks.

Safety Precautions
Willow bark lacks the antiplatelet properties that acetyl has and should not be used in cardiovascular patients for its blood-thinning effects or as an aspirin substitute (Bone and Mills, 2013).

References
Bone, K. A. and Mills, S. (2013). Principles and practice of phytotherapy. New York, NY: Elsevier.

Dalziel, C. (2021). "How to make homemade rooting hormone with willow." *Attainable Sustainable.* Retrieved from https://www .attainable-sustainable.net/rooting -hormone/.

Kuhn, M. A., and Winston, D. (2008). *Herbal therapy & supplements: A scientific and traditional approach.* Philadelphia, PA: Wolters Kluwer/ Lippincott Williams & Wilkins.

BLACKBERRIES, RASPBERRIES, AND DEWBERRIES
(*Rubus* spp.)
Rose Family (Rosaceae)

Description

Blackberries, raspberries, and dewberries are brambles and are known as weedy plants that grow in pastures, fields, edges of woods, and streams. You never see just one in the wild. They are always in a tangle and spread in all directions. The easiest way to recognize them is by their thorny stems, which reach out and grab the passerby, hanging on tightly. To go forward when in their grip is inviting trouble, due to their backward directed bristles. The only way out is to back out. It's one of nature's defenses, protecting the juicy fruits from being easily devoured. But if you're willing to risk a few scratches or tears, they are well worth the effort.

The best time to scout an area for blackberries, sometimes called wineberries, is in May when they are blooming. Dewberry is the earliest bloomer in those areas where it grows. They are similar to blackberry but grow closer to the ground, being more of a creeper than growing upright. They like moist woods and clearings. Blackberry and raspberry follow soon after.

Flowers of the genus *Rubus* have five petals when they bloom and are usually white, but in some species may be pink. The leaves of all the brambles are compound, consisting of three or more toothed leaflets. Younger stems are often referred to as canes. The fruits consist of many small, juicy drupelets, each containing a hard seed. Blackberries and dewberries look very similar, turning black when ripe. Raspberry fruits may be red or black when ripe, depending on the species, and differ from dewberries and blackberries in that they separate from the fleshy stalks when picked, forming hollow shells.

Preparation and Uses

Blackberries, raspberries, and dewberries can all be eaten raw straight from the vine. Dewberries are generally less abundant than blackberries or raspberries. They reach their peak at the hottest and driest time of the year, early- to mid-July, at a time when we need juices for hydration and sugars for energy. The berries can be used to make cobblers, pies, or preserves, and can also be frozen to use during the winter months. The leaves can be used to make tea.

Blackberry Brandy

A spirited drink to share with friends.

- 2 cups fresh blackberries, crushed
- 3 cups Irish whiskey
- 1½ cups sugar syrup (boil 1 cup water with 2 cups organic cane sugar for 5 minutes)

Add crushed berries and 2 cups whiskey to a mason jar. Shake well. Let sit for one week. Pour through a strainer and add the remaining whiskey and sugar syrup.

Medicinal Benefits

Tannin is a natural ingredient found in blackberries, raspberries, and dewberries, making them astringent. The astringent action of the tea made from the leaves reduces intestinal inflammation and helps to relieve diarrhea. Pregnant women sometimes use raspberry leaf tea during their pregnancy to relieve morning sickness and other discomforts (Duke, 1997). Rosemary Gladstar (2008) recommends 1 teaspoon of blackberry root tincture every hour for diarrhea.

Chemical Constituents

Blackberries contain vitamin C, flavonoids, pectin, and fructose. Calcium, magnesium, and flavonoids are found in the leaves (Kuhn and Winston, 2008). Blackberries are also an excellent source of anthocyanins, compounds that have antioxidant and anti-inflammatory properties.

Growing Brambles

Brambles, including blackberries, raspberries, and dewberries are aggressive weeds but tend to be short-lived. Growing them in a contained area is recommended. They can be easily started from sprouts from the parent plant.

Safety Precautions

Thorns are sharp and can inflict painful puncture wounds. A pair of gloves with the fingertips cut out can help.

Sustainability

Brambles need a place to grow. They begin appearing in the second stage of succession after an area has been cleared and along the edges of forests from seeds dropped by birds. Allowing patches to remain wild will give brambles an opportunity to grow. Blackberries and raspberries only produce fruit on the second year's growth so if you want fruit let them grow for another year. It takes dewberries several years to produce fruit.

References

Duke, J. A. (1997). *The green pharmacy.* Emmaus, PA: Rodale Press.

Gladstar, R. (2008). *Rosemary Gladstar's herbal recipes for vibrant health.* North Adams, MA: Storey Publishing.

Kuhn, M. A., and Winston, D. (2008). *Herbal therapy & supplements: A scientific and traditional approach.* Philadelphia, PA: Wolters Kluwer/ Lippincott Williams & Wilkins.

BLUEBERRIES AND HUCKLEBERRIES
(*Vaccinium* spp., *Gaylussacia* spp.)
Heath Family (Ericaceae)

Description

Blueberries and huckleberries get interchanged a lot. Both are native shrubs that have blue or black berries that are edible and sweet and juicy. The easiest way to distinguish between the two is by the seeds. Huckleberries have about ten seeds that are hard and like pebbles. Blueberries are full of soft, tiny seeds.

Blueberries can be grouped into two kinds, the highbush and lowbush. The highbush blueberry can grow up to fifteen feet tall. This is the ancestor of our cultivated blueberry and a common shrub in the eastern United States. Leaves are oval-shaped with green or sometimes red stems that are somewhat zigzagged, making them easy to identify in the winter. It begins flowering as early as April with small white to pale pink bell-shaped flowers. Fruits begin ripening by the end of May. Lowbush blueberries are much smaller, usually no more than three feet high with equally sweet berries. The foliage of both highbush and lowbush turns brilliant red in the fall.

Huckleberries grow one to three feet tall and form colonies. Small, oval-shaped leaves turn shades of orange and crimson in the fall. Flowers range from white to pink or sometimes reddish in the spring and are followed by purplish-black fruits in mid-summer.

Preparation and Uses

Once a blueberry or huckleberry has been recognized and identified, no other description or explanation is really necessary. You simply eat it. Sweet and tasty, blueberries can be eaten raw, added to pancakes, cookies, cakes, pies, or whatever you feel inspired to create.

Blueberry Fizz

A refreshing sparkling drink for that hot summer afternoon.

- 1 cup wild blueberries, chopped in blender or food processor
- ½ cup wild rose petals
- 1 cup sparkling water
- Maple syrup or other sweetener to taste

Cover blueberries and rose petals with cold water and infuse for 12 to 24 hours. Strain and add sparkling water. Sweeten with maple syrup or other sweetener to taste.

Chemical Constituents

Blueberries and huckleberries contain anthocyanosides, arbutin, tannins, flavonoids, and pectin.

Medicinal Benefits

Anthocyanosides contribute to visual acuity and offer protection against ulcers. Arbutin is a compound that is both an antibiotic and a diuretic that helps relieve excess water retention. Other compounds prevent bacteria from adhering to the bladder walls, thus preventing bladder infection.

Growing Blueberries and Huckleberries

Blueberries are easy to grow, require almost no care, and are naturally resistant to disease and insect infestation. Huckleberries are difficult to transplant and do best when grown in a pot for the first couple of years. Once established, they form a colony.

BUGLEWEED
(Lycopus virginica, L. americana)
Mint Family (Lamiaceae)

Description
Bugleweed is a perennial herb that grows in moist, shady soils and wetlands. Tiny white flowers form dense clusters in whirls around a square stem where the leaves join the stem in late summer and early autumn. Leaves are opposite, often purple-tinged, and sharp-toothed.

Part Used
Aerial parts

Preparation and Uses
Leaves and flowers can be used to make a tea or tincture.

Medicinal Benefits and Energetics
Bugleweed is astringent and used for coughs, as a mild sedative, and for hyperthyroidism (Foster and Duke, 2000).

Growing Bugleweed
Bugleweed likes moist conditions in shade or part shade.

Safety Precautions
Not for use in pregnancy or lactation. Avoid using bugleweed if you have hypothyroidism or thyroid enlargement (AHPA's Botanical Safety Handbook, 2013).

References
AHPA's Botanical Safety Handbook, 2nd ed. (2013).

Foster, S. and Duke. (2003). *Eastern/central medicinal plants and herbs.* New York, NY: Houghton Mifflin Co.

BURDOCK
(*Arctium minus, A. lappa*)
Aster Family (Asteraceae)

Description
Burdock is a biennial that is a native of Europe and has naturalized throughout much of the United States. Burdock develops large, broadly heart-shaped basal leaves the first year, usually late summer when their seeds from the previous year have been dispersed. The seeds have hooks and attach themselves to animals, getting tangled up in their fur. The animals then unknowingly distribute these seeds along the trail. In the spring, a flower stalk emerges and may reach from three to six feet tall before it blooms in midsummer with dense clusters of tiny purplish florets. The flower heads have bracts with hooks that curve inward and turn into a prickly burr, somewhat resembling a thistle.

Parts Used
Roots, leaves, stalk, and seeds

Harvesting and Preparation
Burdock is food and medicine. Young leaves are bitter greens and can be cooked through a couple of changes of water before eating. The first-year roots are edible once peeled. After that, they get tough and woody. Burdock sometimes gets mowed down or dies back before it blooms but it will develop another rosette of leaves and continue to send up a flower stalk the next year. Burdock roots go deep into the earth. Use a digging fork or long shovel to remove them. The root is prepared by scrubbing, peeling, then slicing it to add to soups, teas, or other vegetables. The flower stalk, before it has bloomed, can be peeled and nibbled raw or added to salads. Seeds can be collected after the burs have dried and turned brown.

Medicinal Benefits
Burdock is a bitter herb that stimulates the secretion of digestive enzymes. It is used as an alterative for skin conditions, cancer, arthritis, and obesity (Kuhn and Winston, 2008). They are detoxifying as a diuretic and a diaphoretic.

Chemical Constituents
Burdock roots contain protein, lipids, and inulin (Kuhn and Winston, 2008). They are also a source of calcium, phosphorus, and potassium. According to Jim Duke (2007), burdock also contains arctigenin, a lignan found in the seeds and roots that has demonstrated cytotoxic effects against certain types of leukemia.

Growing Burdock
If you want to harvest tender roots, try growing burdock by planting seed in partially shaded, rich, loamy soil in the early spring. Water moderately until it has established itself. Once established, burdock will continue to reseed.

Safety Precautions
Once burdock has attached to an animal, it's difficult to remove and must be cut out.

References
Duke, J. A. (2007). *Herb-A-Day*. Virginia Beach, VA: Eco Images.

Kuhn, M. A., and Winston, D. (2008). *Herbal therapy & supplements: A scientific and traditional approach*. Philadelphia, PA: Wolters Kluwer/ Lippincott Williams & Wilkins.

CATTAILS
(*Typha latifolia, T. angustifolia*)
Cattail Family (Typhaceae)

Description

Cattails are a common sight in wetlands. They grow in open, marshy areas, often in solid stands. Cattails have long, narrow leaves that arise from the base of the plant in the early spring. They are flat and bluish gray in appearance. Flower stalks then develop in mid-spring. Cattails have male and female cylindrical flower buds, both enclosed in a papery sheath, with the male flowers above the female. After the male flowers have released their pollen, the male spike breaks off, leaving behind a female spike that looks like a hot dog on a stick. When the seeds are mature, cottony masses of wind-dispersed seeds are released.

Parts Used

Roots, shoots, flower buds, and pollen

Harvesting and Preparation

Near the base of most cattail stalks, look for a white-pointed sprout that is about one to four inches long. This will be next year's growth. The starchy sprouts and rhizomes are edible. Sprouts can be eaten raw. Rhizomes, however, require processing through pounding and several changes of water to extract the starch for a flour substitute. Young cattail shoots, when about two to three feet tall, can be peeled to the inner core for the heart that is edible raw and can be added to salads. Male flower buds, before the pollen is released, can be steamed like corn on the cob and eaten off the spike. When the male flowers turn yellow and a light tap sends yellow dust into the air, the pollen is ready. The easiest way to collect cattail pollen is to place a resealable bag around the spike and strip the pollen into the bag. The pollen can then be added to cornmeal to make cattail pollen cakes.

Cattail and Thistle Salad

Serve on a bed of wild salad greens for a nutritional and tasty salad.

- 1 cup cattail stalks (inner stem), chopped
- 1 cup thistle stalks, peeled and chopped
- ½ red onion, chopped
- 1 cayenne pepper, chopped
- 1 tablespoon wild herb seasoning
- Salt to taste
- Organic balsamic vinegar

Combine cattail and thistle stalks, red onion, cayenne pepper, wild herb seasoning, and salt. Pour vinegar over vegetables and marinate for at least 30 minutes before serving.

Taste

There is a big difference between the taste of the shoots of the narrow-leaf cattail and the common. The narrow-leaf has almost no taste and is quite bland while that of the common cattail has a refreshing cucumber-like taste. Cattail pollen is very similar in taste and texture to cornmeal.

Precautions

Only harvest cattails from water that is not polluted. If in doubt, boil the cattails for ten minutes before eating them.

Nutritional Benefits

Cattails provide protein, carbohydrates, calcium, magnesium, phosphorus, potassium, sodium, and other important vitamins and minerals.

CHICKWEED
(Stellaria media)
Pink Family (Caryophyllaceae)

Description
Chickweed is an annual herb that starts making an appearance in late summer and early fall in garden beds, lawns, and disturbed areas. It is native to Europe but has become widely naturalized throughout temperate regions. It will continue to grow through the winter unless the temperatures drop below freezing for an extended period of time. It is most abundant in late winter and early spring when it starts to flower. Soon after it flowers, it goes to seed and dies back, forming a weedy mat in its place.

Chickweed is easy to recognize. It is a weak-stemmed plant that comes up in late autumn in mild climates and grows throughout the winter, sprawling across the ground or draping over the pot it has invaded. Its leaves are small and grow in pairs on the stem. Its flowers have five white petals that are deeply notched, giving them the appearance of having ten petals.

Parts Used
Aerial parts

Preparation and Uses
Chickweed leaves, stems, and flowers are all edible and can be eaten raw in salads, in pesto or herb spreads, chopped and infused with water as a tea or infused with a fixed oil to make a salve for inflamed or itchy skin conditions, and added to soups. It can also be tinctured with vinegar to use as a marinade or salad dressing.

Chickweed Vinegar
An excellent way to extract minerals from greens.

- 2 cups chopped chickweed
- 2–3 cups organic apple cider vinegar (enough to cover the chickweed)
- 1 tablespoon honey, optional

Place the chickweed in a jar and cover with apple cider vinegar. Add honey if desired. Cover with a plastic or glass lid or use parchment paper between the chickweed vinegar and a metal lid. Store in a pantry for 2 to 4 weeks. Strain and add to salads, cooked greens, or vegetables.

Nutrients
Chickweed is both food and medicine. It is high in many nutrients, including calcium, phosphorus, magnesium, potassium, and vitamin C. Chickweed has a reputation of being a weight-reducing herb by regulating water levels and driving off excess dampness and fats (Wood, 2009).

Chemical Constituents
Chickweed's chemical constituents include saponins, coumarins, flavonoids, and triterpenoids. Energetically, chickweed is cooling and moistening. As a demulcent, it is soothing and protects irritated or inflamed tissue. Chickweed is a mild expectorant and can be used to treat coughs due to dry and irritated lungs and to move mucus stuck in the lungs. It can also be used as an antirheumatic, vulnerary, and emollient (Hoffman, 2003). Inflamed skin conditions can be relieved with a fresh poultice or an infused oil or salve.

References
Hoffman, D. (2003). *Medical herbalism: The science and practice of herbal medicine.* Rochester, VT: Healing Arts Press.

Wood, M. (2009). *The earthwise herbal: A complete guide to new world medicinal plants.* Berkeley, CA: North Atlantic Books.

CLEAVERS
(Galium aparine)
Madder Family (Rubiaceae)

Description
A common herb that catches your attention is cleavers, also known as bedstraw, an introduced annual. This herb originally come from Europe and has become naturalized throughout most of the United States. The time to start looking for cleavers is in the early spring when the days start getting warm. Cleavers will literally reach out and grab onto you as you pass by. Its leaves and stems are both covered in small, fibrous hairs with tiny hooks on the end, enabling them to stick to clothing and other objects. Cleavers is also one of the few wild greens that has leaves in whorls with six to eight slender leaves forming a circle around its square stem. In the spring, tiny white flowers with four petals appear in the leaf axils followed by tiny, bristly fruits.

Parts Used
Leaves, flowers, and stems

Preparation and Uses
The leaves and stems of cleavers are both edible and medicinal. Chopping them in a juicer, blender, or grinder is the easiest way to prepare them. The chopped leaves and stems can be made into a tea or cooked as greens. They can also be tinctured using alcohol or vinegar. The vinegar can be added to salads or as a marinade for vegetables. The fruits can be roasted to make a stimulating coffee-like beverage.

Green Smoothie with Cleavers
A tasty and nourishing spring tonic.

- 2 cups chopped cleavers
- 1 frozen banana
- 1 cup pineapple or orange juice
- 1 carrot

Place all ingredients in a blender and blend until smooth. Serve immediately.

Medicinal Benefits and Energetics
Cleavers has a long history of use as a medicinal herb. As a diuretic, it is useful for bladder and kidney inflammation and edema. This herb is also cooling and can be useful for hot, stagnant conditions. As a juice or poultice, it can be used for burns, including sunburns. Cleavers move lymph and are therefore beneficial for swollen lymph glands, including tonsils, armpits, breasts, and groin (de la Foret, 2020).

Chemical Constituents
Cleavers contain plant acids, coumarins, iridoids, and tannins (Hoffman, 2003).

Growing Cleavers
Cleavers prefer shady to partly sunny conditions and will volunteer in yards or gardens that have shady edges with moist, leafy soil. If you want to introduce the herb to your yard or garden, look for seeds to mature late spring and into the summer, depending on the area where you live. Cleavers can be sown directly into the garden as soon as its seeds are ripe. When the conditions are right, they will germinate.

References
de la Foret, R. (2020). *Wild remedies.* Carlsbad, CA: Hay House, Inc.

Hoffman, D. (2003). *Medical herbalism: The science and practice of herbal medicine.* Rochester, VT: Healing Arts Press.

CORN SALAD
(*Valerianella radiata, V. locusta*)
Honeysuckle Family (Caprifoliaceae)

Description

Corn salad, also known as lamb's lettuce and mache, is an annual herb that is found during the winter months. The native species and the introduced species are very similar in taste and appearance. Both species of corn salad grow in bunches low to the ground with a rosette of basal leaves.

Leaves are spoon-shaped with smooth margins and round at the top that may reach up to six inches in length. The flowers are small with five white or bluish-white petals. The petals sit in small, flat clusters at the top of forked stems with a pair of stalkless leaves at the fork.

Preparation and Uses

Winter is the time to look for and harvest corn salad. It can be found in open, disturbed areas including fallow fields, garden beds, clearings, and forest openings from New England to North Carolina. Look for it in fields beneath dried grasses and flower stalks from the previous year. As soon as the days start warming up, corn salad blooms and goes to seed, not to be seen again until late fall, when once again it reappears.

Nutritional Benefits and Energetics

Corn salad leaves taste very much like leaf lettuce with a crispy, mildly sweet, nutty taste. Like lettuce, it is also cool and moistening. Traditionally it was used as a salad herb from late autumn to early spring, but corn salad can also be used as a base for other spicy, pungent, or bitter herbs such as wild mustards, cresses, or dandelions. Low in calories and high in nutrients, corn salad is a great herb to know and harvest in the winter at a time when we need vitamins. Corn salad contains vitamins A, C, E, B6, iron, manganese, boron, and potassium. It enhances immunity against infections, helps to prevent macular degeneration, lowers blood pressure, and slows down the aging process.

Growing Corn Salad

Corn salad is easy to grow as a leaf vegetable. All it needs is a sunny spot and disturbed soil with good drainage. The previous year's garden plot is an excellent spot to scatter seeds in September and harvest throughout the winter. Corn salad's delicate nature makes it more desirable raw rather than cooked.

Wild Salad Mix

- Corn salad leaves
- Bittercress leaves and flowers
- Wild mustard flower buds
- Garlic mustard leaves
- Peppergrass/shepherd's purse leaves and flowers
- Dandelion leaves
- Oil and vinegar dressing (optional)

Toss herbs. Add dressing if using and serve.

CRABAPPLE
(*Malus* spp.)
Rose Family (Rosaceae)

Description

Apples come in all shapes, sizes, and colors. Regardless, you know an apple when you see one. The same is true of crabapples. They look just like apples, only smaller, up to one-and-a-half inches in diameter. Crabapples are shrubs or small trees that are armed with stout thorns on the branches and trunks. They grow in the understory of the forest or along the edges of fencerows or abandoned fields where they sometimes form thickets. In the spring, clusters of flowers with five pink petals are borne on the branches. These blossoms are edible and can be added to salads or made into teas.

Apples are native to Europe and Asia and were brought to the United States and domesticated after the arrival of the Pilgrims. Apples were so liked by the Indians that many large orchards existed long before settlers arrived (Erichsen-Brown, 1979). While most crabapple species have been domesticated, there are several that are native to this country. *Malus coronaria* extends from New York west to northeast Arkansas and south to northern Georgia. *Malus angustifolia* is a southern species and is found from Virginia south to northern Florida and west to Louisiana. *Malus ioensis* is the prairie crabapple and grows from northern Indiana south to Arkansas and Oklahoma and north to southeastern South Dakota. On the west coast is the Oregon crabapple, *M. fusca*.

Narrow-Leaf Crabapple
(*M. angustifolia*)

The narrow-leaf crabapple of the southeast is totally lacking in sweetness, but what it lacks in sweetness it makes up for in pectin, especially in the skin. Because of their high pectin content, narrow-leaf crabapples can be used as a source of pectin when making jams or jellies from fruits that are low or lacking in pectin. A liquid pectin can be made from this crabapple and stored for later use.

American Crabapple (*M. coronaria*)

Fruits are a dark greenish-yellow and tart.

Chemical Constituents

Pectin is a soluble fiber and has been used both for diarrhea and for constipation (Duke, 1997). In addition to pectin, crabapples contain B vitamins, small quantities of vitamin C, rutin, a large number of minerals, organic acids, tannin, enzymes, and various substances (Couplan, 1998).

Sustainability

The narrow-leaf crabapple is considered threatened in some states due to loss of habitat. Allow crabapples to grow and plant seeds from wild species when possible.

References

Couplan, François. *The Encyclopedia of Edible Plants of North America*. New Canaan, CT: Keats Publishing, 1998.

Duke, J. A. (1997). *The green pharmacy*. Emmaus, PA: Rodale Press.

Erichsen-Brown, C. (1979). *Medicinal and other uses of North American plants: A historical survey with special reference to the eastern Indian tribes*. Mineola, NY: Dover Publications, Inc.

North Carolina State Extension. "Malus angustifolia." Retrieved from https://plants.ces.ncsu.edu/plants/malus-angustifolia/.

North Carolina State Extension. "North Carolina Extension Gardener Plant Toolbox." Retrieved from https://plants.ces.ncsu.edu/plants/malus-angustifolia/.

DANDELION
(Taraxacum officinale)
Sunflower Family (Asteraceae)

Description
Dandelions are one of the most common and recognizable wild greens. It is an early bloomer and one of the first wildflowers to make an appearance in the spring. Dandelions are perennials and one of the first wildflowers to bloom, beginning in late winter and continuing into the spring with yellow heads of very small, aggregated flowers. It has a basal rosette of leaves that remain present through the winter in milder climates but will die back if the temperatures drop below freezing for a period of time. Its smooth, dark green leaves are deeply lobed with pointed tips. The fruits are slender brown nutlets attached to a parachute that sails them through the air to reseed. The root is a taproot and grows deep into the ground.

Parts Used
All parts

Harvesting and Preparing
In late winter or early spring when dandelions are just beginning to bloom, the flowers are at their best. They become more bitter as the days get warmer. Leaves can be harvested any time they're available. Younger leaves are more tender and less bitter, but these are also available during the summer. They are continuously growing new leaves except during the winter, especially if it's a cold climate. The harvest season for roots is late fall and into the winter unless the ground is too frozen to dig.

Dandelion-Coconut Macaroons (gluten-free)

- 2 cups gluten-free pancake mix
- 1 cup coconut flour
- 1 cup cane sugar
- 4 cups dandelion flower petals (separated from green base)
- ½ cup butter
- ½ cup coconut oil
- 4 eggs
- 1 teaspoon vanilla

Combine pancake mix, coconut flour, and sugar with the dandelion flowers. Cream together butter, coconut oil, and eggs. Stir in vanilla. Drop by rounded teaspoonfuls onto oiled cookie sheet. Bake at 350°F for 10 minutes.

Nutritional and Medicinal Benefits
Dandelion is ranked among the most nutritional green vegetables. The leaves contain vitamins A and C, potassium, calcium, iron, phosphorus, and B vitamins. Dandelion is a cooling, bitter herb used for digestion and as an aperitif to stimulate the appetite (Bone and Mills, 2013). Autumn-harvested roots contain inulin, a natural prebiotic that nourishes the gut (The Herbal Academy, 2017). The whole plant is used for detoxification. Dandelion stimulates the production of bile in the liver that helps to digest fats, producing a slight laxative effect. It is also a diuretic and detoxifies by flushing toxins out through the urine.

Chemical Constituents
Dandelions contain triterpenes, carotenoids, flavonoids, and polysaccharides (Hoffman, 2003).

Growing Dandelions
Give them space. All dandelions need is a sunny spot or part shade.

Look-Alikes

Young leaves of dandelion look very similar to the young leaves of hawkweed (*Hieracium* spp.), wild lettuce (*Lactuca* spp.), and sow thistle (*Sonchus* spp.). Dandelion differs from the others in that it only has one flower per stem.

References

Bone, K. A. and Mills, S. (2013). *Principles and practice of phytotherapy*. New York, NY: Elsevier.

Hoffman, D. (2003). *Medical herbalism: The science and practice of herbal medicine*. Rochester, VT: Healing Arts Press.

The Herbal Academy. (2017). "All about dandelion." Retrieved from https://theherbalacademy.com /dandelion-materia-medica/.

ELDER
(Sambucus canadensis)
Moschatel Family (Adoxaceae)

Description

Elder is a native, deciduous shrub or small tree with representatives throughout the United States. It grows at the edges of forests, fields, hedgerows, and swamps, forming a large crown with its spreading branches. Finding elder is easy. It starts blooming in May and can be spotted while driving down the road by its large, flat-topped clusters of small white flowers that appear in late spring. These flowers have five petals that are about a quarter-inch wide and mildly fragrant. They are followed by purple-black berries, which ripen during the summer months. Elder leaves are pinnately compound with five- to eleven-toothed leaflets growing in pairs.

Parts Used

Flowers and ripe berries

Preparation and Uses

Flowers are best harvested as they begin opening on dry, sunny days. They can be dried on a rack and infused in hot water to make tea or used fresh to make a beverage. Before the flowers have completed their blooming cycle, the berries begin developing first as little green balls that gradually turn red, then deepen to a purple, and finally turn almost black before they are finally ripe. The berries can be harvested mid to late summer when they have turned bluish black in color. Dry elderberries in clusters on a rack for a couple of days before de-stemming. They break loose more easily when dried. The dried berries can then be used to make syrup, jelly, shrubs, or desserts.

> ### Elderflower Syrup
> *A cooling, refreshing drink*
> *for a hot summer day.*
>
> - 2 cups elderflowers
> - 1 lemon, sliced
> - 8 cups organic cane sugar
> - 5 cups water
>
> Place flowers and sliced lemon in a large bowl and set aside. Bring sugar and water to a boil and continue to cook for 5 minutes. Pour sugar water mixture over flowers and lemon slices and blend together. Store in a cool, dark place for several days. Strain. Use to sweeten lemonade or add sparkling water for a cooling summertime drink.

Medicinal Benefits

The flowers are anti-inflammatory, antiviral, anti-catarrhal, and diaphoretic. The berries are also antiviral and anti-inflammatory and can be used for coughs and colds and for flu prevention. Elderflowers are considered blood movers and are good for clearing heat and toxins, as with eczema or other skin conditions. Elderflower tea can be used to reduce inflammation and for skin eruptions (Hobbs, 2013).

Chemical Constituents

Elderflowers contain flavonoids that include kaempferol, quercetin, and rutin. The berries contain anthocyanin, vitamin C, and malic acid (Kuhn and Winston, 2008).

Growing Elder

Elder tolerates a wide variety of soil conditions but does best in rich, moist soil. Cuttings can be taken from underground rhizomes that send up shoots. Elder will produce more fruit if it gets a lot of sunlight.

Safety Precautions

All parts are considered poisonous except for the flowers and berries. Unripe berries, mostly the seeds, may cause nausea and diarrhea when eaten raw in large amounts. Dried and cooked berries are nontoxic (Kuhn and Winston, 2008). The red-berried elder (*S. pubens*) is considered poisonous. Elder grows in moist, swampy areas, the same habitat as water hemlock (*Cicuta maculata*). Both are shrubs with white-topped clusters of flowers and compound leaves, but water hemlock is deadly. No room for a mistake.

Sustainability

The biggest threat to elder is habitat. They grow along the edges of ditches and in hedgerows, both of which are frequently cleaned out and mowed. Scatter elder seeds in wild, damp areas to help spread the population.

References

Hobbs, C. (2013). *Grow it heal it: Natural and effective herbal remedies from your garden or windowsill*. New York, NY: Rodale Press.

Kuhn, M. A., and Winston, D. (2008). *Herbal therapy & supplements: A scientific and traditional approach*. Philadelphia, PA: Wolters Kluwer/ Lippincott Williams & Wilkins.

EVENING PRIMROSE
(Oenothera biennis)
Evening Primrose Family (Onagraceae)

Description and Habitat
Evening primrose is a native biennial that is common throughout the United States in fields, waste places, and backyards. Evening primrose comes up from seed in late summer or early fall and forms a basal rosette of leaves that remain green through the winter. The long, narrow leaves lie flat on the ground and are often speckled with red spots. The next spring, as the days get warmer, a flower stalk develops from the center of the rosette and by early  summer it reaches up to eight feet in height. By mid-summer, pale yellow flowers with four petals form at the top of the stalk. They open in the early evening as the sun goes down. The lowermost flowers open first and remain open through the night and into the morning. As soon as the sun hits them the next morning, they droop. By midday, all the flowers droop, and new ones open the next evening. After the flower petals drop, the four-chambered seed capsule starts developing, containing numerous little black seeds. The capsule is pale green at first, then starts turning brown as the seeds mature.

Preparation and Uses
Evening primrose leaves, seeds, and roots are all edible. The seeds generally germinate in the fall after they have dropped from the parent plant. As soon as the leaves have developed, they can be picked and added to salads or cooked as greens throughout the winter. During the winter when most plants are dormant, the taproot is growing, accumulating starch and sugar to feed the emerging second-year stem. This root can be peeled, chopped, and boiled for 20 to 30 minutes as a cooked vegetable or added to soup. The root is slightly pungent and sweet which adds a hint of spiciness to your food. Flowers can be eaten raw or added to salads. Following the flowers are the seeds. After the seed capsules have matured and started turning brown, cut the flower stalk, turn the plant upside down in a paper bag, and let the seeds drop into the bag. Breaking up the individual capsules releases the remainder of the seeds. Store them in a jar and use them throughout the year by grinding and adding them to cooked vegetables, soups, or stir-fries.

Evening Primrose Vinegar
A mild-tasting dressing for salads or vegetables.

- 4–5 medium-size evening primrose roots and leaves, chopped
- 1 teaspoon fresh turmeric, chopped
- 2 fresh cayenne peppers, halved lengthwise
- 1 teaspoon evening primrose seeds
- 1 teaspoon honey
- 2 cups rice vinegar

Place evening primrose, turmeric, and peppers in a quart jar. Add honey and cover with vinegar. Put a lid on the jar and store in a dark, closed pantry for at least 2 weeks.

Medicinal Benefits
Evening primrose seeds contain tryptophan, an amino acid that helps the body produce serotonin, a mood elevator that can enhance the feeling of well-being.

Chemical Constituents
The oil from the seeds, dried leaf, flower, and root bark is rich in gamma-linoleic acid (GLA) that reduces inflammation and hypertension (Kuhn and Winston, 2008).

Growing Conditions
Evening primrose is easy to grow from seed and can be transplanted during the first year. Scattering the seeds around the edge of a garden or herb bed in late summer will almost certainly result in plants coming up the following fall or spring.

References
Kuhn, M. A., and Winston, D. (2008). *Herbal therapy & supplements: A scientific and traditional approach.* Philadelphia, PA: Wolters Kluwer/Lippincott Williams & Wilkins.

FIELD GARLIC
(*Allium vineale, Allium* spp.)
Amaryllis Family (Amaryllidaceae)

Description
Field garlic is easy to spot in a field or yard during the winter months. The wispy grass-like leaves stand above other plants and are commonly referred to as onion grass. Field garlic has leaves with parallel veins that run from the tip to the base without any branching. Field garlic and wild onions are often confused. Field garlic grows in clumps but has  tough, thin leaves and a papery brown sheath covering a bulb that is divided into cloves. Wild onions have bulbs. Leaves of the field garlic are hollow and branch off the main stem. Leaves of the wild onion are flat, not hollow, and emerge from the base of the plant. Both are distinguished from other plants by their garlic odor when crushed. The flowers develop as rounded clusters at the tip of the stem and are purplish to a greenish white with three sepals and three petals. Instead of fruits, they have bulblets.

Uses
All parts are edible, including flowers, leaves, bulblets, and underground bulbs. They are used to add spice to our food. Its roots can be used as a substitute for onions and garlic and its tops can be used like chives. Marinating in a honey or sugar mixture with water can mellow the taste. Field garlic is great for adding a pungent flavor to soups and vegetable dishes. It grows through the winter and in the spring sends up a flower stalk. The bulbs can be dug and used anytime they are visible. But the bulbs are largest and at their best just before they bloom in the spring. They can be hung in bundles and air-dried and used as needed. They can also be infused with vinegar for use as a salad dressing or marinade.

Nutritional and Medicinal Benefits
Field garlic is an excellent source of vitamin C, vitamins A and B, and is rich in sulfur, iron, and calcium. But field garlic is more than just food. If it smells pungent like garlic, it's food medicine. The strong pungent smell can be attributed to sulfur compounds that have antimicrobial activities (Pengelly, 1996). It is also a diaphoretic, hypotensive, and antispasmodic (Hoffman, 2003).

Constituents
Garlic contains organosulfur compounds as well as enzymes including alliinase, B vitamins, minerals, and flavonoids.

Growing Garlic
Just let it grow. Garlic occurs naturally in most areas and reproduces by underground bulbs and aerial bulblets.

References
Hoffman, D. (2003). *Medical herbalism: The science and practice of herbal medicine.* Rochester, VT: Healing Arts Press.

Pengelly, A. (2004). *The constituents of medicinal plants.* Cambridge, MA: CABI Publishing.

GOLDENROD
(Solidago spp.*)*
Sunflower Family (Asteraceae)

Description
Solidago is a genus of ninety to one hundred and ten species. The preferred one among many herbalists is sweet goldenrod (*S. odora*) due to its anise flavor. However, any of the members of the genus *Solidago* can be used interchangeably. Goldenrods average one to four feet but the taller species can reach eight feet and bloom in late summer with a spike of white to yellow flowers. Goldenrod is often mistakenly believed to cause hay fever; the real offender is ragweed that blooms at the same time. Goldenrod pollen is heavy and can only be transported by insects while the tiny molecules of ragweed pollen are transported by wind and aggravate allergies.

Parts Used
Goldenrod flower heads and leaves can be harvested when the flowers are at their peak. At the same time, avoid any leaves or flowers that are brown or have mildew.

Uses
An extraction of leaves and flowers can be used to make a tea or tincture. This could be helpful in the early phase of an allergic reaction when the body is sneezing, has watery eyes, and a runny nose. Sweet goldenrod (*S. odora*) has anise-like properties that add a nice flavor to tea in addition to its other benefits.

Medicinal Benefits and Energetics
Goldenrods are astringent and dry up excessive mucus secretions. According to Foster and Duke (2000), goldenrod leaf tea is used for a number of ailments, including diaphoretic, diuretic, colds, and coughs. It is useful for acute or chronic upper respiratory congestion and to reduce phlegm (Hoffman, 2003).

Chemical Constituents
Goldenrod constituents include saponins, essential oils, and flavonoids (Winston, 2016).

Growing Goldenrods
Goldenrods grow in a broad range of soils, light, and moisture. Collect the seeds in the fall and scatter them where you want them to grow.

Safety Precautions
Goldenrod may cause allergies, although most allergies attributed to goldenrod are actually due to ragweed pollen.

References
Foster, S. and Duke. (2003). *Eastern/central medicinal plants and herbs*. New York, NY: Houghton Mifflin Co.

Hoffman, D. (2003). *Medical herbalism: The science and practice of herbal medicine*. Rochester, VT: Healing Arts Press.

Winston, D. (2016). "The worst weeds are your best medicine: The common and weedy plant material medica." Lecture notes from 2016 Medicines from the Earth.

GROUND CHERRY
(Physalis spp.)
Nightshade Family (Solanaceae)

Description
There are a number of species of *Physalis*, both native and non-native, that are found throughout the United States. Most of these species are edible, but some are grown as ornamentals, known as Chinese lanterns, and are not edible. Ground cherries usually grow in open, sunny edges of fields, gardens, and other disturbed  areas. Ground cherries are most easily recognized when they produce fruits. Also called husk tomatoes, they look like cherry tomatoes with a papery husk surrounding them, giving the appearance of a miniature lantern. The papery husk is actually an inflated calyx formed by sepals enclosing the berry and is unique to this genus, making it easy to identify. The berry color ranges from greenish-yellow, orange, or red, depending on the species. Depending on the species, the leaves may be alternate or opposite with mostly smooth margins. Ground cherry flowers are pale yellow or white with five cup-shaped petals.

Preparation and Uses
Only the ripe fruits are edible. When the papery husk starts turning tan or brown, the fruits are ready. The ripe fruit has a similar feel as a ripe tomato. Ripe fruits can be used in the same way as cherry tomatoes to make pies, sauces, and other dishes. They keep well when dried in their papery husk for a short period.

Ground Cherry Vinaigrette
This vinaigrette adds a tangy, tomato-like flavor to your food.

- ⅔ cup ground cherries, pitted and halved
- 1 tablespoon fresh basil, chopped
- 2 fresh cayenne peppers, halved lengthwise and seeds removed
- 1 jalapeno pepper
- ½ cup organic balsamic vinegar or enough to cover the herbs
- Salt to taste

Put all ingredients in a blender. Chop coarsely. Serve over pasta or as a dressing or marinade.

Constituents
Ground cherries contain physaline, a bitter principle. They also contain vitamin A, vitamin C, minerals, tannin, and mucilage (Couplan, 1998).

Safety Precaution
Unripe fruits and leaves contain solanine and other solanidine alkaloids that could be toxic. The Chinese lantern, *P. alkegengi*, has red bladders and is cultivated for decorative and ornamental value but sometimes escapes into the wild.

References
Couplan, François. *The Encyclopedia of Edible Plants of North America*. New Canaan, CT: Keats Publishing, 1998.

GROUNDNUTS
(Apios americana)
Pea Family (Fabaceae)

Description

Not a nut at all, groundnuts are actually legumes that grow as a climbing vine around the stems of trees, shrubs, and other plants in the area. It is the underground tuber that gives it the name groundnut. The tubers grow on a long string just below the surface of the soil.

A native herbaceous vine, groundnuts live along the edges of banks, streams, and moist meadows and thickets. The narrow, egg-shaped leaves are compound with five to seven leaflets, pointed at the tip with smooth margins. Most of the year, the groundnut blends in with the vegetation around it until it blooms mid-summer. At that time, clusters of maroon-colored, pea-shaped flowers develop in the leaf axils, followed by long, green pods with edible seeds that look and taste like peas.

Preparation and Uses

Groundnut seeds can be cooked and eaten like peas. Their roots are a source of protein and can be cooked and eaten like potatoes. The tubers grow on a string just below the surface. The outer skin is somewhat tough and is easier to peel after boiling in water for about ten minutes. Slice and add to soups, vegetables, or as a potato substitute.

Groundnut Soup

A hearty and robust soup to enjoy on a cold winter day.

- ¼ cup field garlic, chopped (or 1 medium onion, chopped)
- 2 carrots, chopped
- 1 stalk celery, chopped
- 1 cup groundnut tubers, peeled and sliced
- 1 quart chicken or vegetable broth
- 1 tablespoon dried nettles
- Cayenne pepper to taste

Sauté garlic or onion in a skillet until tender. Add carrots, celery, and groundnuts and cook on medium heat for about 10 minutes. Transfer to a larger pot and add broth and seasonings. Cook on medium-low heat for 20 to 30 minutes. Serve with rice.

Nutritional Benefits

Groundnuts contain three times as much protein as potatoes.

Growing Groundnuts

Groundnuts are easy to grow if you have a pond or wet area. Plant tubers along the edges of creeks, rivers, or ponds in part sun in the fall.

Safety Precautions

Groundnuts grow along the edges of marshes and wet areas where snakes are numerous. Watch your step when harvesting.

Sustainability

When harvesting groundnuts, break off the larger tubers and replant the smaller ones for next year. Replanting the smaller tubers can ensure that you will be able to return to the same spot year after year to harvest groundnuts.

HAZELNUT
(Corylus americana)
Birch Family (Betulaceae)

Hazelnuts are familiar to most people as coffee, cookies, and nut butters. Most of these hazelnut products are made from the European hazelnut (*Corylus avellana*), also known as filberts, but hazelnuts have also been introduced in North America and are grown commercially here.

Description
Hazelnuts are shrubs that can reach a height of up to ten feet. They grow in thickets and along the edges of woodlands and ditch banks across the northern United States and southern Canada. Their leaves are somewhat heart-shaped, alternate, and have double teeth along the margins. The female flowers are small and easy to miss. They are about a quarter inch across with only the pistils showing, projecting in all directions from their buds, and are located above the male catkins. This tends to prevent pollination from occurring on the same plant. Instead, they rely on the wind for cross-pollination.

The beaked hazelnut, *C. cornuta*, lives along both coasts, whereas the American hazelnut, *C. americana*, is limited to eastern North America. It is easy to distinguish between the two species by the husks. The beaked hazelnut is named for the bristly husk that resembles a tube-like beak at its tip. The husk of the American hazelnut looks more leaf-like and is ragged on the end. The beaked hazelnut has smooth twigs, while the twigs and leafstalks on the American hazelnut are covered with rough hairs.

Preparation and Uses
The nuts of both shrubs are delicious raw or cooked. Harvest hazelnuts as soon as they start turning light brown in late summer. Remove the outer hull and spread out on a tray to dry. Once they are dry, lightly crack the nut and shell out the nutmeat within. Use in cookies, pies, cakes, or any recipe calling for nuts. Hazelnuts are high in oil and should be shelled and frozen to prevent them from going rancid.

Growing Hazelnuts
Hazelnuts can be grown successfully from seed by planting in the ground in the fall. Young seedlings can also be transplanted with success.

Sustainability
Populations have declined due to loss of habitat. Encourage their growth by planting them in the shade of other trees and giving them space.

HICKORY
(Carya spp.)
Walnut Family (Juglandaceae)

Description
There are seventeen varieties of hickory trees, thirteen of which are native to the United States. They live in the eastern and southern parts of the country. Hickories are tall trees, usually found in older, mature forests where the understory is open, allowing for easy walking and visibility. In the fall, the compound leaves (made up of five to nine leaflets, depending on the species) turn golden yellow and light up the forest floor with a warm glow as they fall to the ground. When the hickory nut matures, the outer husk splits into four separate chambers and the nut drops to the ground. This happens about the same time the leaves turn yellow and drop.

Shagbark hickory (*Carya ovata*) and shellbark (*C. laciniosa*) are considered by many to be the best, but all are edible. Some just taste better than others. Fruits from the familiar pecan tree (*C. illinoensis*), a native hickory grown in the southeast, have been commercialized and used widely in the United States. It's a good practice to crack and taste a nut before gathering a large quantity.

Preparation and Uses
Gathering hickory nuts is the fun part. Later comes the tedious part of sorting and removing any that are discolored or have grub holes. Wash them to remove any dirt or debris and spread out on a flat tray to dry. Once you have gotten the nuts home, the nutshell must then be cracked to get to the nutmeat inside.

Cracking hickory nuts requires skill that comes with practice. Unlike pecans, the shell surrounding the nutmeat is hard and can only be opened with a rock or hammer. Once the nut is shelled, either use right away or freeze. The high content of oil can cause them to go rancid in a short while. The unshelled nuts can be stored for a longer period of time, but they too will go rancid after about a year, so be sure to do the sniff test before eating them.

Shelled hickory nuts can be used in pies, puddings, and cakes. Nuts can also be crushed and boiled. The nutmeat floats to the top, which can be skimmed off, and the heavier shells sink to the bottom. The strained liquid, or nut milk, can be used as a drink or added to bread, cookies, or cakes to add a nutty flavor.

Sap from hickories is edible and can be collected in the early spring. Drill a half-inch hole into the base of a tree and insert a spigot into the hole. Use a bucket or tie a plastic bag around the spigot to collect the liquid. It can be boiled down to make a mildly sweet syrup in the same way as maple sap.

Nutritional Benefits
Hickory nuts are very nutritious. According to the USDA, one pound of shelled hickory nuts has more than three thousand calories and three hundred grams of fat, including essential fatty acids shown to prevent heart disease. They also provide protein, carbohydrates, iron, phosphorus, and trace minerals.

Growing Hickory
Hickory trees grow slowly, sometimes not producing nuts until they are eighty years old. If you're going to grow hickory, look for seedlings and be prepared to wait. Pecans mature much more quickly and can be a good alternative.

Sustainability
Hickories grow in mature forests. Allowing forests to remain forests will contribute to the growth of hickory trees. Planting seedlings in young forests will give them an opportunity to grow with the forest.

HORSEMINT
(Monarda punctata)
Mint Family (Lamiaceae)

Description

Horsemint, also called horse balm, is a short-lived perennial or biennial of the mint family. It blooms in late summer with yellowish, purple-dotted flowers that grow in whorls in the upper leaf axils with white or pale purple bracts at their base.

The square stem and opposite leaves are characteristic of the mint family and may grow up to four feet tall. Horsemint grows in sandy soil in maritime forests, dunes, clearings, and fields. There are other species of *Monarda*, also commonly known as horsemint, that grow over most of the United States and southern Canada.

Preparation and Uses

Leaves and flowers can be used to make tea or a substitute seasoning for thyme and oregano.

Herbal Mouthwash

Leaves the mouth feeling clean and refreshed.

- ½ ounce horsemint tincture
- ½ ounce prickly ash tincture
- ¼ ounce peppermint tincture
- 4 drops goldenseal tincture
- 3 drops peppermint essential oil

Combine ingredients and add to 8 ounces of water. Use as a mouthwash to promote healthy gums.

Medicinal Benefits

Research studies have shown that carvacrol helps prevent the breakdown of acetylcholine, a compound that seems to be lacking in people with Alzheimer's disease. Since horsemint contains 1.25 percent carvacrol, it seems probable that it could be an effective medicine against Alzheimer's disease (Duke, 1997). Thymol is antiseptic and anti-fungal (Hoffman, 2003).

Chemical Constituents

Carvacrol and thymol

Growing Horsemint

Horsemint is easily propagated from seed, which can be collected during the fall and winter months. The seed head looks similar to the cultivated bee balm and can be grown by scattering those seeds where you want them to grow.

References

Duke, J. A. (1997). *The green pharmacy.* Emmaus, PA: Rodale Press.

Hoffman, D. (2003). *Medical herbalism: The science and practice of herbal medicine.* Rochester, VT: Healing Arts Press.

INDIAN PIPE
(Monotropa uniflora)
Heath Family (Ericaceae)

Description
Indian pipe is an ethereal-looking plant that grows on the forest floor. Believed to be a mushroom or fungus by many who first encounter it, Indian pipe is actually a native perennial wildflower related to blueberries and can be found in forests where there are mushrooms. They have a relationship with the fungi that have a relationship with the trees under which they grow. Together they form a network.

Indian pipe lacks chlorophyll and therefore is not green. The white, sometimes pink color stands out on the forest floor. A single, translucent stem with scaly bracts emerges from the decaying plant material with a nodding, bell-shaped flower that resembles a clay pipe. The petals have four to five petals and a single pistil in the center with ten to twelve stamens (Knopf, 1979).

Parts Used
The whole plant can be used to make medicine. However, it is best to leave the roots and take only the tops unless the plant is abundant.

Preparation and Uses
Indian pipe is more of a medicine than a food. The taste is earthy. A tincture can be made of the entire plant, including the roots. Some people prefer to use only the root, some the aerial parts only, and others the root and the aerial parts. The plant should be tinctured while it is fresh.

Benefits
Indian pipe is considered to be a pain reliever, antispasmodic, diaphoretic, and sedative (Duke and Duke, 2016).

Safety
There hasn't been a lot of research done on Indian pipe, so start with a low dosage and monitor how it makes you feel.

Sustainability
Indian pipe grows in the woods so loss of habitat is its biggest threat. Avoid trying to transplant Indian pipe. When harvesting, take only the top part to allow the root to continue to send up new growth the next season.

References
Duke, J. A. and Duke, J. (2016). *Useful plants of the Catoctin: Blue Ridge of Maryland*. Virginia Beach, VA: Eco Images.

Knopf, A. A. (1979). *The audubon society field guide to North American wildflowers: Eastern region*. New York, NY: Alfred A. Knopf.

LINDEN
(Tilia americana)
Mallow Family (Malvaceae)

Description

Linden, also known as basswood, is a native deciduous tree with large, somewhat heart-shaped leaves with lopsided bases, and sharply toothed margins. The aromatic flowers are small with five creamy white to pale yellow petals. Most distinctive is the leaf-like bract, attached to the flower stalk for about half its length. The fruit is a nut-like capsule. When fresh, it has a mucilage, sweetish taste.

Preparation and Uses

The flowers, with the bracts, make a tasty, refreshing beverage.

Linden Tea

Linden makes an excellent cold-water or hot tea.

A cold infusion takes longer but has a fresher, more flowery taste. For a cold-water infusion, pack a quart jar with approximately 1 ounce of fresh linden flowers. Cover the flowers with cold water and let it sit overnight. Strain the water from the flowers. Strain and drink. Sweeten to taste.

For a hot infusion, pour hot water over 2 to 3 tablespoons of linden flowers. Steep 10 minutes or longer, strain, and drink. Sweeten to taste.

Medicinal Benefits

The flowers can be tinctured and used for medicinal purposes. Linden has been widely used for its gentle sedative effects and for restlessness, especially in children and for nervous tension (Mills, 1991). Linden is a diaphoretic and diuretic and is used for feverish colds, flus, and other respiratory infections (Foster and Duke, 2000).

Chemical Constituents

Linden flowers are mucilaginous and contain sugar, tannin, flavonoids, and a volatile oil, to which their fragrant odor is due (Henriette's Herbal Homepage, 1995–2020).

Growing Linden

Linden is a larger tree and needs plenty of room to spread its branches. Seedlings can be planted from spring to early fall in both partial or full sun locations. Linden trees grow best in well-drained, moist, fertile soils, but are very adaptable to less than favorable conditions.

References

Foster, S. and Duke. (2003). *Eastern/central medicinal plants and herbs*. New York, NY: Houghton Mifflin Co.

Henriette's Herbal Homepage. (1995–2020). "Tilia—Linden flowers." Retrieved from www.henriettes-herb.com/eclectic/kings/tilia.html.

Mills, S. Y. 1991. *Out of the earth: The essential book of herbal medicine*. London, England: Viking Arkana.

MALLOW
(Hibiscus spp.*)*
Mallow Family (Malvaceae)

"Whosoever shall take a teaspoon of the Mallows shall that day be free from all diseases that may come to him."

—Pliny, Roman author, naturalist, and natural philosopher

Description
At the peak of summer, when the sun's rays are the most intense and the temperatures climb to record highs, the mallows bloom. Marshes become dotted with pinks and whites of several species of the mallow family, the same family that includes okra, hibiscus, hollyhock, cotton, and about fifteen hundred other species that grow throughout the world. Mallows are fairly easy to recognize with five petals and a center that looks like a bottlebrush from the way the stamens are attached to the sides of the pistil. None are poisonous and most have been used as food by early cultures.

Common Mallow *(Malva neglecta)*
Common mallow is a non-native trailing plant that can be found throughout the country. It grows in lawns, vacant lots, and cultivated gardens. Its leaves are round with shallow lobes and toothed edges. Although the leaves of common mallow are edible, the rough texture of the leaves may make them scratchy on the throat. Cooking them softens them and brings out a mucilaginous feeling. Small pale pink flowers with five petals develop in the summer months and are arranged in clusters along the branches. Circular, flat fruits that resemble a miniature wheel of cheese develop from the flowers. The fruits are sometimes referred to as cheeses due to their shape.

Rose Mallow (*Hibiscus moscheutos*)
Rose mallows are one of the most common native mallows in the United States, mostly found in freshwater marshes. They are large, herbaceous perennials, reaching heights of three to eight feet by the end of summer with large heart-shaped leaves. From July to September, rose mallows produce large, showy flowers, with usually white but occasionally pink petals. Following the flowers are the fruits, which are five-parted capsules containing seeds within the chambers. The fruits of the rose mallow are larger than those of the common mallow. Rose mallow fruits measure up to 2 inches in length.

Parts Used
Fresh or dried leaves, flowers, flower buds, fruits, and roots have all been used as food or medicine.

Preparation and Uses
Flower petals are mild tasting and crunchy and can be added to salads or teas. Mallow leaves, especially when they are young and tender, can be eaten raw in salads or cooked as a potherb. The leaves are mucilaginous and give a thickening quality to vegetable dishes or casseroles. They can also be dried and ground to a powder and used in soups and teas. Young fruits are tender and mild tasting and can be added to salads, stir-fries, or cooked vegetables. The fruits of rose mallow are similar to okra in taste and texture, only smaller. Gather the fruits while young. Just like okra, they get tough within a couple of days after they have started developing. During the winter, mallow tops die back but underground the mucilaginous root is still alive and growing. This is the time to gather roots. Scrub the roots, then chop and dehydrate them to make teas. Because of the mucilage content, a cold-water infusion is suggested. Put roots in a jar, cover with cold water, and let sit overnight.

Wild Vegetable Stir-Fry with Mallow Fruits
A tasty summer dish packed with nutrition.

- Olive oil, for sautéing
- 1 medium onion
- 1 green pepper
- 1 cayenne pepper
- ½ cup rose mallow fruits, halved, ends removed
- ½ cup ground cherry fruits
- 1 cup fresh purslane, chopped

To a sauté pan heat oil, add vegetables, and cook on medium heat for 10 to 15 minutes. Serve with rice.

Nutritional Benefits and Energetics

Mallow leaves are loaded with beta-carotene, iron, calcium, and essential fatty acids (Tashel, 1994). They also contain phosphorus and vitamins A and C. The taste is mostly bland but slimy. Mallows are cooling and are soothing to the respiratory, digestive, reproductive, and urinary systems (Weed, 2007). They act as a demulcent and emollient in dysentery and lung and urinary ailments (Foster and Duke, 2000).

Chemical Constituents

Mallow leaves and roots contain large quantities of mucilage (Foster and Duke, 2000). Hibiscus flowers provide calcium, manganese, potassium, and vitamin C as well as flavonoids (Weed, 2007).

Growing Mallows

Mallows are easy to grow in their preferred habitat. A number of the Hibiscus species are wetland plants so they need a pool or low wet area. Common mallows come up in yards and gardens. If you don't have them, they are easy to introduce by transplanting or scattering seed.

Safety Precautions

Even though the roots of most mallows are edible or medicinal, those of the cotton (*Gossypium* spp.), also in the mallow family, are not.

References

Foster, S. and Duke. (2003). *Eastern/central medicinal plants and herbs*. New York, NY: Houghton Mifflin Co.

Tashel, C. (1994). "Mallow—the wonder weed." Santa Fe Botanical Gardens newsletter, Vol. 2, No. 3, September 1994.

Weed, S. (2007). "Herbal adventures with Susun Weed: The malvaceae or mallow family." Retrieved from http://www.susunweed.com/herbal_ezine/November07/wisewoman.htm.

MULBERRY
(Morus rubra, M. alba)
Mulberry Family (Moraceae)

Description

Often described as the tree with blackberries, mulberries are medium-size trees with fruits that look like blackberries. In southeastern Virginia, there are at least two species of mulberry: red mulberry and white mulberry. They ripen before blackberries, usually mid to late May.

Red Mulberry

The red mulberry is a native and has large, ovate leaves that have a long-pointed tip and three main veins arising from the base. The leaves are rough above with soft hairs beneath. The female flowers are tiny and clustered together. The red mulberry eventually sprouts berries that are made up of many one-seeded fruits, turning red to dark purple when ripe.

White Mulberry

The white mulberry is a native of China and was introduced as a host plant for the silkworm caterpillar. The leaves are shiny green above and paler and slightly hairy beneath. The fruits may be white, red, or black. They may possibly hybridize with the red mulberry.

Preparation and Uses

Ripe fruits can be eaten raw, made into pies, preserves, wine, or cordials. Fruits can be dried and ground to a powder to use in cooking to add sweetness to a dish.

Mulberry Preserves
A tasty topping for desserts and breads.

- 2 cups fresh mulberries
- 1 cup organic cane sugar

Place mulberries in a pan and add sugar. Bring to a gentle boil, stirring to dissolve the sugar. The berries will make their own juice. Boil rapidly for 10 to 15 minutes, stirring frequently. Pour into mason jars and seal.

Medicinal Benefits

The taste of the red mulberry is sweet, while the taste varies among white mulberries. Some are sweeter than others. The fruit has properties that are anti-inflammatory, antioxidant, and nutritive (Winston, 2016).

Chemical Constituents

The fruit contains anthocyanins and malic acid (Winston, 2016).

Growing Conditions

Mulberries germinate readily from seeds dropped by birds. They can successfully be transplanted into the landscape and will thrive in either sun or part shade.

Safety Precautions

Eat in moderation. Large quantities may have a laxative effect.

References

Winston, D. (2016). "The worst weeds are your best medicine: The common and weedy plant material medica." Lecture notes from 2016 Medicines from the Earth.

MULLEIN
(*Verbascum thapsus*)
Figwort Family (Scrophulareaceae)

Description and Habitat
Mullein is a non-native species that was introduced from Europe but has since naturalized and now grows throughout the United States. Mullein is easy to spot when driving down the road in mid-summer. The flower stalk stands straight and tall, towering above all the other plants growing around it. Mullein is a biennial. The first year it forms a basal rosette of velvety leaves that are covered with irritating hairs. The second year it sends up a flower stalk that may reach six feet tall with a spike-like cluster of small, five-petaled yellow flowers.

Parts Used
Leaves and flowers

Preparation and Uses
Mullein leaves are best harvested the second year before the flower stalk starts developing. The leaves can be used fresh or dried, alone, or with other herbs to make a tea for coughs or asthma. Mullein leaves are often mixed in with smoking mixes to treat coughing, sore throat, asthma, and other bronchial-related issues. A tincture can also be made with mullein leaves, preferably fresh. Chop the leaves into small pieces, pack into a quart jar, and cover with a high-proof alcohol, making sure the herb is covered right up to the top. Cover and let sit for at least two weeks.

Mullein flowers can also be used fresh or dried to make a tea, oil infusion, or tincture. When making an oil infusion, use dried or wilted flowers, cover with olive oil, and let sit for four to six weeks. For a mullein flower tincture, pack a pint jar with flowers, cover with 50 percent alcohol, and store in a dark pantry for four to six weeks.

Herbal Smoking Mix
Make your own nicotine-free smoking blend for that after-dinner smoke.

- 4 ounces mullein (*Verbascum thapsus*) leaves
- 3 ounces life everlasting (*Pseudognaphalium obtusifolium*) leaves and flowers
- 3 ounces passionvine (*Passiflora incarnate*) leaves
- 2 ounces yaupon (*Ilex vomitoria*) leaves
- 2 ounces mugwort (*Artemisia* spp.)
- 1 ounce wild lettuce (*Lactuca canadensis*)

Grind and mix the herbs together.

Medicinal Benefits
Mullein leaves and flowers are an expectorant, demulcent, anti-catarrhal, vulnerary, and mildly analgesic and are beneficial to the respiratory system as a decongestant (Bone, 2003). The leaves are cooling, moistening, and relaxing, especially to the lungs. Leaves can also be used as a poultice for swollen glands, bruises, insect bites, and other minor ailments. An extract of mullein flowers in olive oil is soothing to inflamed areas and for ear problems (Hoffman, 2003).

Chemical Constituents
Mullein leaves are high in mucilage. Mullein contains flavonoids, mucilage, saponins, and tannins (Hoffman, 2003).

Growing Mullein
Mullein reproduces and spreads by seeds. Scatter mullein seeds in a cleared, sunny area where they can grow without danger of being sprayed or mowed. They grow well in poor soil that hasn't been fertilized. When the plants emerge, weed around them so that they don't get crowded out.

Safety Precautions

The leaves are covered with fine, irritating hairs that can cause a rash and may cause irritation during the processing (de la Foret, 2021). Contrary to what many believe, mullein leaves do not make good toilet paper. Those irritating hairs will leave you unable to sit for a week. Be sure to strain your tea through fine muslin to remove any irritating hairs. Other than that, there are no known contraindications or side effects. Avoid harvesting near roadways or areas that have been sprayed. Those fine hairs collect and trap pollutants.

Look-Alike

The young leaves of mullein look very similar to lamb's ear (*Stachys byzantine*), which is also medicinal but has different properties and uses.

Sustainability

Mullein is a prolific seed producer and produces an abundance of seeds that can remain viable in the soil for up to one hundred years. If you cut the leaves and tops off before it produces seed and leave the root, it will come back each year.

Mullein is considered an invasive species by the National Park Service and is threatened by the introduction of two insects, a European curculionid weevil and a mullein moth that are specific to mullein (Plant Conservation Alliance's Alien Plant Working Group, 2005).

References

Bone, K. A. (2003). *A clinical guide to blending liquid herbs: Herbal formulations for the individual patient.* St. Louis, MO: Churchill Livingstone, An Imprint of Elsevier, St. Louis, MO.

de la Foret, R. (2021). "The Mullein Plant." *Herbs with Rosalee.* Retrieved from https://www.herbalremediesadvice.org/mullein-plant.html.

Hoffman, D. (2003). *Medical herbalism: The science and practice of herbal medicine.* Rochester, VT: Healing Arts Press.

Plant Conservation Alliance's Alien Plant Working Group. (2005). "Fact sheet: Common mullein." Retrieved from https://www.invasive.org/weedcd/pdfs/wgw/commonmullein.pdf.

NETTLES
(Urtica dioica, Laportea canadensis)
Nettle Family (Urticaceae)

Description
Nettles are herbaceous perennials. There is a native species and a non-native species. The non-native species, *Urtica dioica*, most often referred to as stinging nettle, was introduced from Europe and is the one most commonly encountered in gardens. In some areas it has escaped cultivation and grows wild. Nettles are often found by touch rather than sight. Their leaves and stems are covered with tiny hairs that are like hypodermic needles, injecting fluids under the skin that cause a stinging sensation. The length of time of the stinging sensation varies with individuals. Some hardly even notice it, while others may feel its effects for several days. On rare occasions, someone may have an allergic reaction.

Stinging Nettles *(Urtica dioica)*
Stinging nettle grows upright with branching stems. Its leaves are oval shaped with toothed margins and a pointed tip. Long clusters of small, whitish flowers hang from the leaf axils. There are both male and female plants, but only the females produce seeds.

Wood Nettles *(Laportea canadensis)*
The native species, known as wood nettle, grows in moist woodlands, shady seeps, and other moist, shady areas. Its leaves are much larger than the European species. Both the leaves and stems are covered with stinging hairs. Both the male and female flowers are greenish white. The male flowers develop in the axils of the leaves while the female flowers develop near the top of the plant.

Parts Used
Leaves, roots, and seeds

Preparation and Uses
Nettle is both food and medicine. Leaves should be gathered in the spring before they bloom and can be used fresh or dried for later use as a green vegetable, in soups, spreads, or infused in hot water for tea. Cooking nettles breaks down the stingers so that you can ingest them without being stung. They naturally restore energy levels and can be used for detoxification, to relieve allergies, and to strengthen bones, hair, nails, and teeth.

Nettle Pesto
A tasty way to enjoy your vitamins.

- 4 cups fresh nettle greens
- 1 cup toasted pecans
- 1 cup extra-virgin olive oil
- 6 cloves garlic
- 1 teaspoon herb seasoning
- Juice from 1 lemon
- ½ cup parmesan cheese

In a blender or food processor, process all ingredients except the Parmesan cheese. Add the Parmesan cheese and blend until smooth. Serve on crackers, pasta, or your favorite bread.

Nutritional and Medicinal Benefits and Energetics
Nettle is salty, cooling, and drying. As a food it is highly nutritive, adding lots of vitamins and minerals, including calcium, manganese, magnesium, vitamin K, carotenoids, and protein to the diet (de la Foret, 2020). Jim Duke suggests a daily dose of nettle leaf tea for seasonal allergies, including hay fever and pollen-related concerns. Injections of histamine from the stinging nettle for arthritis and rheumatism have provided relief for those who have tried it (Duke, 2007). Nettle leaves and roots are a diuretic and detoxify by flushing toxins out through the urine. An extract of the root has been used with success for benign prostatic hyperplasia (Duke, 2007). Herbalist David Winston has found nettle seed to be effective in treating the kidneys (Winston, 2012). Jonathan Treasure uses nettle seed extract for kidney protection (Treasure, 2018).

Chemical Constituents
Fresh leaves of stinging nettle contain histamine, acetylcholine, formic acid, and serotonin (Kuhn and Winston, 2008).

Growing Nettles

Nettles spread by underground rhizomes and are easy to grow by division. They prefer moist, partly shady conditions and will quickly colonize.

Safety Precautions

Fresh nettles sting when brushed against and cause rashes if touched. Wear gloves when harvesting nettles. Nettles may also decrease the efficacy of anticoagulant drugs.

References

de la Foret, R. (2020). "Nettle Herb." *Herbs with Rosalee*. Retrieved from https://www.herbal remediesadvice.org/nettle-herb.html# :~:text=Herbalist%20David%20Winston%20 has%20popularized%20the%20use%20 of,trophorestorative%20–%20literally%20 a%20food%20for%20the%20kidneys)

Duke, J. A. (2007). *Herb-A-Day*. Virginia Beach, VA: Eco Images.

Kuhn, M. A., and Winston, D. (2008). *Herbal therapy & supplements: A scientific and traditional approach*. Philadelphia, PA: Wolters Kluwer/ Lippincott Williams & Wilkins.

Treasure, J. (2018). "Case history: Nettle seed & kidney function." Retrieved from http: //jonathantreasure.com/evidence-research -testimonials-case-history/case-histories /nettle-seed-kidney-function.

Winston, D. (2012). "Little-known uses of common medicinal plants." American Herbalists Guild.

OAKS
(Quercus spp.)
Beech Family (Fagaceae)

Description

Oaks are the givers of life. They spread their branches out to nurture you and provide a buttress to nestle into. Its fruits are life sustaining and its bark is healing. There are many types of oaks with more than three hundred species, not counting the hybrids. Oaks are mostly deciduous trees that occur in the temperate, subtropical, and rarely tropical regions in the northern hemisphere (Weakley, Ludwig, and Townsend, 2012).

Oak leaves are alternate and vary in shape with lobed, toothed, or straight edges. Its bark is light gray and scaly or blackish with furrows. Spring brings with it male and female flowers. The male flowers are small with yellowish-green catkins that are about two to three inches long and on the same twig as the female flower. The female flowers are inconspicuous with red styles and a short, stubby, green stalk that sits in the leaf axils. The fruit is an acorn with a cap for its outer hull.

Oaks are basically divided into two groups, although the dividing line is not always clear. There are red oaks, with veins extending beyond the margins of the leaves and nuts that mature in two years. There are also white oaks, with smooth margins on the edges of the leaves and nuts that mature in one year.

Harvesting

Acorns mature and begin dropping from trees in the fall. The initial drop is often immature acorns that are shed by winds and storms. They will taste more bitter than the ripe ones. Wait for them to take on a shiny, ripe look to gather them.

Beetle Larvae

When gathering acorns, look for the ones that have a small, round hole drilled into them and remove them. The hole was likely drilled by a female acorn weevil that has a long snout for drilling. Then, she lays 2 to 4 eggs that hatch as larvae and feed on the nutmeat (Unger, 1999).

Preparation and Uses

The nuts of the white oak group are low in tannins and can be eaten straight from the tree when mature. The nuts of the red oak group are extremely bitter and astringent when eaten raw due to the presence of tannins. They can be transformed from a bitter, astringent nut to a sweet, nutty-tasting food by soaking them in water until the water turns dark from the tannins. Pour the water off and repeat the process until the water is clear. Using cold water often produces better-tasting nuts and works best if the acorns are shelled and ground first. Using hot water doesn't necessarily require shelling and grinding them first and speeds up the process. Once the tannins have been removed, they can be ground and used as flour or eaten as nuts.

Acorn Cookies
A cookie packed with nutrition and flavor.

- 2 cups acorn meal
- 1 cup pancake/biscuit mix
- ¼ cup coconut flour
- ¼ cup almond meal
- ¼ cup cocoa powder
- 1 cup organic cane sugar
- 1 stick butter, melted
- 3 eggs
- 1 teaspoon vanilla
- ½ cup honey

Mix dry ingredients together. In a separate bowl, mix butter, eggs, vanilla, and honey. Add to dry ingredients. Blend well. Drop by spoonsful on an oiled cookie sheet. Bake at 350°F for 15 minutes.

Nutritional Benefits

The astringency of white oak bark makes it especially useful for getting rid of diarrhea or dysentery. Its tannins are anti-inflammatory and antiseptic (Hoffman, 2003). It was traditionally used as a gargle for sore throat and a wash for skin eruptions, poison ivy, rashes, and burns

(Foster and Duke, 2000). A tea can be made by decocting 1 teaspoon of bark in 1 cup of water, bringing to a boil, and simmering for 10 to 15 minutes (Hoffman, 2003). A lukewarm solution of the tea forms a seal that can protect the skin against infections (Mills, 1991).

Chemical Constituents

All oaks contain tannins. They are found in the bark, the nuts, and in oak galls. Tannins are one of the main plant constituents responsible for astringency.

Growing Oaks

Growing an oak tree is easy. All you need is dirt and a seed and a place to let it grow. If it is a member of the white oak group, it will start to germinate within a few days. Sometimes the root starts to develop while still on the tree. If you put them in a plastic bag and leave them for a few days, they will sprout. Plant these in the ground or in a pot and next spring they will send up new growth. Oaks from the red oak group germinate the following spring (Tallamy, 2007).

Sustainability

Oaks grow in old forests and many old forests are disappearing. Plant an oak tree whenever you can.

References

Foster, S. and Duke. (2003). *Eastern/central medicinal plants and herbs*. New York, NY: Houghton Mifflin Co.

Hoffman, D. (2003). *Medical herbalism: The science and practice of herbal medicine*. Rochester, VT: Healing Arts Press.

Mills, S. Y. 1991. *Out of the earth: The essential book of herbal medicine*. London, England: Viking Arkana.

Tallamy, D. W. (2007). *Bringing nature home: How native plants sustain wildlife in our gardens*. Portland, OR: Timber Press.

Unger, L. 1999. Acorns for Rent. UK Department of Entomology. Retrieved from http://www.uky .edu/Ag/Entomology/ythfacts/allyr/yf804 .htm.

Weakley, A. S., Ludwig, J. C., & Townsend, J. F. (2012). *Flora of Virginia*. Fort Worth, TX: Botanical Research Institute.

PASSIONVINE
(Passiflora incarnata)
Passionflower Family (Passifloraceae)

Description

Passionvine is a native herbaceous vine that is common in southern states. It is a fast growing plant that climbs over fences, trees, shrubs, or anything that will support it.

Passionvine has large, deeply lobed leaves with tendrils in the leaf axils. Large, whitish-purple flowers appear during the summer months and are the passionvine's most distinctive characteristic. A fringe of thread-like filaments grows out from the base of the petals and rests on them. Following the flowers are fruits that are actually berries. They look like miniature watermelons when they're green with a thick outer skin that turns yellow and wrinkly as they ripen. Inside the skin is sweet, juicy pulp.

Preparation and Uses

Passionvine leaves, stems, and flowers can be used to make a relaxing tea. The fruits are edible with a sweet, almost grapefruit-like taste. They can be eaten raw as a snack while in the field or juiced to make a refreshing drink.

Sleep-Ade
A relaxing beverage before going to bed.

- 13 grams lemon balm (*Melissa officinalis*)
- 7 grams linden (*Tilia americana*)
- 7 grams passionvine (*Passiflora incarnata*)
- 4 grams skullcap (*Scutellaria lateriflora*)
- 4 grams wild lettuce (*Lactuca canadensis*)

Mix dried herbs in a large bowl. Store in a closed container in a dark pantry.

Tea
Add 4 grams mixed herbs to a cup or tea-pot. Add 1 cup hot water, cover, and let steep for 10 to 15 minutes. Strain and sip slowly.

PAWPAW
(Asimina triloba)
Custard Apple Family (Annonaceae)

Description

Pawpaw is in the custard apple family, a family that is primarily represented in the tropics. Pawpaws are small trees or large shrubs that form patches in the understory of moist woods and stream banks in much of the eastern  United States. They reach their northernmost range in New York and extend west to eastern Texas.

Pawpaw leaves are long and oval shaped and alternate on the stem. Crushed leaves emit a pungent odor unlike any other leaves in the forest. Its brown and fuzzy terminal buds make winter identification easy. In early spring, before the leaves have developed, small button-shaped buds open to form a maroon-colored flower with three triangular petals. Carrion flies, houseflies, and green bottle flies have been observed on the blossoms and flying from one tree to another. Flowers have to be cross-pollinated to produce fruits. Pawpaw fruits grow in clumps of three or four on the branches of the trees and begin to ripen in late August, reaching their peak in mid-September. You can locate the fruits by looking for the long leaves, which turn yellow about the time the fruits are ripening. Fruits are three to five inches long, somewhat oval shaped, and slightly curved. They have a green skin that turns yellow as the fruits ripen later in the summer. The pulp inside is yellowish and soft, like custard. Embedded in the pulp are two rows of large, dark seeds.

Harvesting Pawpaws

Pawpaws drop to the ground when ripe and should be gathered right away before they turn black. If they are not fully ripe, you can place them on a table at room temperature and they will continue to ripen. Sample the fruit for taste when gathering. Flavor varies from tree to tree.

Some are sweet, some have very little flavor, some have a bitter aftertaste, while others are like eating pudding out of the skin.

Preparation and Uses

Pawpaws are best when eaten raw straight from the tree. The skin is easily removed by using a sharp knife to peel it off. You can either pick the seeds out by hand or press the pulp through a sieve. The pulp has been used in much the same way as a banana.

Pawpaw Smoothie
A smooth and delicate taste.

- 2 cups pawpaw pulp
- ½ cup honey
- 1 cup coconut yogurt
- 1 teaspoon vanilla

Place ingredients in a blender. Add ice and purée until smooth.

Nutritional Benefits

Pawpaws are high in vitamin C, magnesium, iron, copper, and manganese. They are a good source of potassium and several essential amino acids. They also contain significant amounts of riboflavin, niacin, calcium, phosphorus, and zinc.

Chemical Constituents

In addition to nutritional value, scientists at Purdue University have found that pawpaws contain compounds that exhibit highly effective pesticidal and anticancer properties. The bark, roots, twigs, and seeds of pawpaw contain certain acetogenins that might help fight cancer cells. The seeds, which are toxic, also have insecticidal properties.

Growing Conditions

Pawpaws do best if they get both shade and sun. They will grow in the shade but will produce more fruit if they get sunlight. They prefer moist, well-drained soil. Pawpaws have a long taproot, making it difficult to transplant them, so it's best to seed them directly into the soil where you want them to grow. Pawpaws form patches from underground rhizomes.

Safety Precautions

Handling the fruit may cause contact dermatitis among sensitive individuals. Seeds are toxic.

PERSIMMON
(Diospyrus virginiana)
Ebony Family (Ebonaceae)

Description

Persimmon is a small to medium-sized tree that grows at the edges of forests, on sand dunes, and hillsides from Connecticut south to Florida and west to eastern Texas. The oval-shaped leaves are three to six inches long with smooth margins. Trees are either male  or female and both are needed to get fruits. The fruits are actually round berries that have three to seven large seeds and are about one to two inches in diameter. They turn orange when ripe and are sometimes mottled with purple.

Harvesting Persimmons

Fall is the best time to harvest persimmons. You know persimmons are ripening when you start finding undigested seeds in the scat of possums and raccoons on the trail. When the fruits turn soft with a somewhat mottled color, they are ripe. In some areas, the ripening of persimmons coincides with the timing of the first frost. However, in the southeast, all the persimmons are gone if you wait for the first frost because raccoons and possums will have eaten them all. When the skin gets wrinkly and turn a mottled purple color, the persimmons are ripe. If they are soft and bubbly, they're overripe and have begun fermenting.

Preparation and Uses

Persimmons look like miniature pumpkins with large seeds embedded in the pulp. The best way to remove the seeds and extract the pulp is with a food mill. Ripe fruits are sweet and edible. Unripe fruits are astringent and cause the mouth to pucker.

Persimmon Scones
Serve with honey-butter spread on top.

- ⅓ cup butter, softened
- 1 egg
- 2 cups biscuit baking mix
- 1 cup persimmon pulp
- 1 teaspoon vanilla flavoring
- ½ cup half-and-half
- 2 tablespoons maple syrup

Combine butter and egg. Add to baking mix. Add persimmon pulp, vanilla flavoring, and half-and-half. Mix ingredients and drop by spoonful on a baking dish. Bake at 350°F for 12 to 15 minutes.

Growing Conditions

Persimmons germinate readily from seed buried in well-drained soil in the fall. They will grow in part shade or sun but will produce more fruit in the sun.

Predicting Winter

Ask the persimmon tree—she will tell you. The secret lies within her seed. Cut the seed in half and inside you will find either a fork, a knife, or a spoon. If it is a fork, you can expect a mild winter with plenty to eat. If it is a knife, it's going to be biting cold, so cold it will cut through you. If it is a spoon, you're going to be shoveling snow.

Safety Precautions

Ripe persimmons attract wasps and hornets that feed on the nectar from the fruits. Practice awareness when harvesting from the ground.

PINE
(*Pinus* spp.)
Pine Family (Pinaceae)

Description and Habitat

Pines are often referred to as the pioneers of the forest. They are one of the first of the woody plants to move into an area that has been cleared or reclaimed by nature. Pines are part of a large family that also includes larches, hemlocks, firs, spruces, and Douglas firs. The genus of pines (*Pinus*) grows throughout most of the United States and is characteristic of acid soils, often sprouting after a fire. Pines are easy to identify by their needle-shaped leaves that are arranged in a bundle-like cluster of two to five needles. Clusters of male flowers, called catkins, develop at the base of new growth with the female flowers, called cones, scattered singly or in small clusters along new shoots. After the flowers are fertilized it takes two, sometimes three, years for the cones to reach maturity (Grimm, 1962).

Parts Used

Pine sprouts, needles, catkins, pollen, and resin

Harvesting and Preparation

Pine seeds germinate readily and come up thick. A small percentage of these seedlings will make it to maturity. This is the time to harvest the seedlings, while they are still young and tender. Break off the root and eat the whole thing or add it to your salad. It gets tough as it gets older.

Male catkins begin developing in early spring. Often referred to as male cones, they are actually the male reproductive parts that release the yellow pollen that is so obvious in the spring. Young catkins have a sweet, citrus-like flavor that becomes bitter as they mature. At this stage they can be infused in honey. They will slowly release their pollen into the honey, enriching the flavor and nutrition.

When you start seeing the first signs of yellow dust in rain puddles, on your car or sidewalk, you know the pollen is ready to harvest. The catkins will go from being green to almost yellow and will become plump, ready to explode. One method of collecting pollen is to use a one- or two-gallon resealable bag, place it over the branch, and shake the pollen into the bag. The pollen can then be siphoned or strained to remove the debris from the catkins and branches. A much easier method is to locate pines with lower branches that need to be pruned. Just before the catkins open, clip off the end branches with the unopened catkins, spread them on a tray in a ventilated, protected area from the wind, and they will release their pollen slowly as they are ready. Leave the catkins on the tray for a couple of weeks, then carefully lift the branches. The pollen should be on the bottom. Strain the pollen through a sifter or strainer to remove unwanted debris.

Pine pollen can be tinctured. When tincturing pine pollen, tincture the entire catkin. Use pure grain alcohol and 30 percent to 40 percent water using a 1:5 ratio of pollen to liquid. Put a lid on the jar and shake well. Store in a dark pantry, shaking daily for two weeks.

Pine resin is the sap that exudes from a pine tree if it has been wounded or damaged. It's the tree's attempt to heal itself. The sap acts as a glue to seal up a wound, and can act the same way on a human wound. When the sap first oozes out from the tree, it is clear and sticky. As it dries, it hardens and takes on an amber-like color. When collecting resin, make sure to leave enough to protect the tree.

Edible and Medicinal Benefits

Pine needle tea is high in vitamin A and vitamin C and has a citrus-like taste. It is an overall tonic that boosts the immune system, prevents respiratory infections, and strengthens heart health among other things. Use kitchen scissors to cut the pine needles into one- or two-inch lengths, add a cup of hot water to a tablespoon of chopped needles, cover, and let steep. The longer it steeps, the stronger it gets.

Pine pollen contains significant quantities of testosterone and other male sex hormones known as androgens and restores androgen/estrogen balance. It stimulates liver regeneration, reduces cholesterol, enhances immunity, and supports healthy endocrine function (Buhner, 2016).

Pine resin is astringent and has antiseptic and anti-inflammatory properties and can be applied to open wounds. The sap is also an effective insect repellent and is used to manufacture pine tar soap, which helps repel insects and prevent poison ivy.

Spring Burst Seasoning
A stimulating burst of flavor that tastes like spring.

- 8 ounces pine pollen
- 8 ounces yaupon matcha
- 16 ounces rosemary matcha

Combine ingredients. Sprinkle on salads, vegetable dishes, or add to herb spreads. Note: Matcha is a finely ground powder of dried herb leaves.

Chemical Constituents
Pine pollen contains sterols, steroid-like substances, as well as protein, carbohydrates, flavonoids, and amino acids. Pine resin contains pinene, one of a group of terpenes, valued for their fragrance, healing properties, and gentle reaction on the skin (Pengelly, 1996).

Growing Pines
Pines can be started from seedlings, but their long taproots make them difficult to transplant. They germinate readily from seeds. Seeds are contained within scales and, for most pines, when the seeds are mature in late summer these scales opens and release the seeds. Most seeds are attached to wings and are dispersed by the wind (Grimm, 1962). These can be collected and planted where you want them to grow. Pines like a lot of sunlight and grow fast once started.

Safety Precautions
Use caution if you tend to have allergies. You may think that you are allergic to pine pollen, but it may be grass pollen instead.

References
Buhner, S. H. (2016). *Natural remedies for low testosterone: How to enhance male sexual health and energy*. Rochester, VT: Healing Arts Press.

Grimm, W. C. 1962. *The book of trees for positive identification*. New York: Hawthorn Books, Inc.

Pengelly, A. (2004). *The constituents of medicinal plants*. Cambridge, MA: CABI Publishing.

PLANTAIN
(Plantago major, P. lanceolata)
Plantain Family (Plantaganaceae)

Description
Plantain is a great plant to know for many reasons. It is edible and medicinal with multiple uses. It is a non-native perennial herb that has worldwide distribution with about two hundred and fifty species. Common and lance-leaved plantains are the two most commonly used.

Common Plantain
Common plantain sends up a narrow greenish-white leafless spike with tiny, inconspicuous flowers. The fruit is a small capsule that splits open around the middle.

Lance-Leaved Plantain
Lance-leaved plantain sends up a long, narrow flower stalk from the center of the basal leaves. A dense head of tiny, inconspicuous flowers grow at the top and are followed by a two-seeded capsule.

Parts Used
Leaves, seeds

Preparation and Uses
Plantain leaves can be infused as a tea or in oil for making therapeutic salves. They can also be tinctured.

Medicinal Benefits and Energetics
Plantain is cooling, mucilaginous, moistening, and astringent (Wood, 2008). The taste is mild. Some may say bland or slightly sweet. A light decoction of a tea made from the plantain leaves can help soothe the digestive and urinary tract (Hobbs, 2013). Plantain leaves are good for drying up dripping sinuses and for allergies. They are expectorant, analgesic, and antimicrobial (Hoffman, 2003). Seeds are rich in mucilage and useful as a laxative and for inflammation of the digestive tract (Gladstar, 2008).

Plantain can also be used for first aid in the field. A spit poultice of the leaves can provide immediate relief to insect bites or infected areas. Leaves infused in a fixed oil can be prepared as a salve, either alone or with other herbs for skin conditions, including poison ivy.

Chemical Constituents
Plantain leaves contain glycosides, terpenoids, polysaccharides, alkaloids, and flavonoids. Seeds contain tannins and fatty acids (Kuhn and Winston, 2008).

Growing Plantain
If you don't already have plantain, seeds are easy to find in mid-summer to early fall. Collect the seeds and scatter them where you want them to grow.

References
Gladstar, R. (2008). *Rosemary Gladstar's herbal recipes for vibrant health.* North Adams, MA: Storey Publishing.

Hobbs, C. (2013). *Grow it heal it: Natural and effective herbal remedies from your garden or windowsill.* New York, NY: Rodale Press.

Hoffman, D. (2003). *Medical herbalism: The science and practice of herbal medicine.* Rochester, VT: Healing Arts Press.

Kuhn, M. A., and Winston, D. (2008). *Herbal therapy & supplements: A scientific and traditional approach.* Philadelphia, PA: Wolters Kluwer/Lippincott Williams & Wilkins.

Wood, M. (2008). *The earthwise herbal, Volume 1: A complete guide to old world medicinal plants.* Berkeley, CA: North Atlantic Books.

PLUM
(*Prunus* spp.)
Rose Family (Rosaceae)

Description

Plums are mostly small trees or shrubs that spread their roots underground and form colonies. There are at least fifteen species spread across the United States, plus a number of other varieties that have hybridized. Plums generally have white flowers in the early spring. The flowers are followed by fruits that begin ripening as early as late May in some areas and as late as August or September in other areas. The fruits come in an assortment of colors ranging from deep purple, red, or yellow. Some taste sweet while others may be tart.

Plums look very similar to cherries and even share the same genus name *Prunus*. Wild native types range from one half to one-and-a-half inches in diameter. The fruits of plums are generally fleshier and the stone in the center is more flattened than those of cherries. Some plum trees have thorns, whereas cherry trees are thornless.

American Plum (*P. americana*)

American plums are probably one of the best-known wild plums and can be found throughout the Midwest and eastern United States. Its fruits turn red when ripe, usually mid to late summer. Somewhat tart in flavor, they make delicious sauces, pies, and other desserts.

Chickasaw Plum (*P. angustifolia*)

Chickasaw plums have a wide range, extending from Texas and Oklahoma in the southwest to Pennsylvania and south to Florida. They grow in dry, sandy soil along roadsides, stream banks, and edges of forests. The fruits turn a peachy color when ripe and have a somewhat tart flavor.

Beach Plum (*P. maritima*)

The beach plum grows along the east coast from southern Maine to Virginia. As its name implies, it grows near the beach, often in pure sand. Fruits turn purplish black when ripe, usually late summer to early autumn.

Harvesting Wild Plums

Like most wild fruits, plums don't all ripen at the same time. It means making repeated visits to the plum patch. When they are ripe, they drop to the ground. They should be gathered soon after dropping to prevent insect invasion and mold. If it feels bubbly when you pick it up, fermentation has begun. Plums can be picked from the branches as long as they fall into your hands. If you have to tug to pull them loose, they probably aren't ripe. It's okay to pick partially ripened plums for additional flavor and pectin.

Preparation and Uses

While most plums are good to eat straight from the tree, the pulp can also be used to make juice, jelly, or preserves.

Growing Wild Plums

Wild plums generally grow in disturbed or abandoned areas. Because of that, they require little care once started. They can be started from seed but, according to growers, germinate more consistently following a cool, moist stratification for three to five months. They can also be divided. Plums spread out and form a thicket, developing roots where the stem goes into the ground. Dig deep enough around the plant to get a good root system. Once planted in the ground, water for several days until it has adjusted.

Caution

The twigs of wild plums are covered with dull pointed thorns so be mindful when picking to avoid getting punctured.

POKE
(Phytolacca americana)
Pokeweed Family (Phytolaccaceae)

Description

Pokeweed is a native perennial that is distributed in the eastern half of the United States, from Minnesota in the north to New England, south to Florida, and west to Texas and Mexico. Its seeds germinate in open, sunny areas. Poke can be found growing in disturbed soils: on the banks of ditches, behind old sheds or other outbuildings, in garbage dumps, and in gardens and plant beds. Hundreds of tiny seedlings poke their way through the surface of the soil as soon as the days start warming. Roots already in the soil send up new shoots, and every year those roots and shoots get larger.

Poke is easier to identify in the fall than in the spring. It starts out with a bright green, succulent stem with oval-shaped leaves that taper at both ends. Sometimes there are red streaks going up the stem, an indicator of the presence of toxic alkaloids. As the plant matures, it may reach a height of up to nine feet before dying back in the fall.

Small white flowers appear in mid-summer followed by purple-black berries that often linger on the plant after its leaves have dropped. By this time the thick stalks have turned a deep red and the branches, loaded with purple-black berries, sprawl out in all directions from the main stem. This is the easiest time to identify poke. Make a mental note of its location and come back in the spring when it emerges once again.

Harvesting and Preparation

Poke is edible, medicinal, and can be poisonous. Harvest poke in the early spring when the shoots first emerge from the soil and are up to one foot tall. Sometimes it is possible to cut the top six to eight inches from the growing plant, as long as there are no red streaks in the stem and it hasn't started to bloom yet.

The young leaves and stalks are edible. Whether you're using leaves or stalks, poke must be cooked before eating. Cover the leaves and/or stalks with cold water. Bring just to the point of boiling. Pour off the water and cover a second time with cold water. Again, bring just to the point of boiling and then drain. It is now ready to eat or include in any recipe that calls for asparagus or cooked greens.

Poke Sallet
A tasty dish packed with nutrition.

- 1 medium onion
- 2 tablespoons butter
- 4 cups prepared young poke greens and stalks, cooked
- 3 eggs
- ¼ cup sour cream
- 1 cup grated cheese

Sauté onion in butter and add poke. Combine eggs, sour cream, and grated cheese. Pour egg mixture over onions and greens. Sprinkle cheese on top. Cover pan and cook on medium-low heat until firm.

Medicinal Benefits

Poke leaves and stem act as an alterative and diuretic. Poke supports the immune and lymphatic system.

Chemical Constituents

Poke contains phytolaccine alkaloids that can cause intense vomiting and diarrhea. The root is the most poisonous part.

Growing Poke

You don't have to grow poke. It grows itself. Just give it a space in your yard or garden, scatter a few berries in the fall, and you will have it.

Safety Precautions

Pokeberries contain mitogens that may cause dermatitis in some people. Using gloves to gather and prepare the young plants can help prevent intense itching later. Children have reportedly been poisoned from eating too many berries or from making poke berry juice and drinking it raw.

PRICKLY ASH
(Zanthoxylum americanum, Z. clava-herculis)
Citrus Family (Rutaceae)

Description
Prickly ash is an aromatic, small tree with spreading branches and stout spines on the trunk. The leaves are compound with five to thirteen leaflets, often with paired spines at the base. Small, yellow-green flowers develop in branched clusters at the ends of twigs in the spring. The fruit is a follicle containing a shiny, black seed. The taste of prickly ash bark, leaves, and follicle is pungent.

Common Prickly Ash
Common prickly ash grows in moist soils in valleys and rocky uplands.

Southern Prickly Ash
The southern prickly ash is a small, aromatic tree that grows along the coast from central Virginia to Florida and west to east Texas in sandy soil. The trunk of the southern prickly ash is armed with stout thorns that resemble teeth.

Parts Used
Inner bark, seed follicles, leaves

Preparation and Uses
The bark can be harvested in the spring or fall. Harvest from side branches rather than the trunk of the tree. Peel the bark and let dry for a few days before cutting it into small pieces to use for a tea or tincture. Seed follicles can be harvested in the late summer while they are still green. Remove the seeds and let dry. Dried follicles can be ground and used as a seasoning. Leaves can also be dried and used as a zesty seasoning.

Zest!
A spicy blend of black pepper, turmeric, and prickly ash

- 1 ounce black peppercorns
- ½ ounce turmeric
- ⅛ ounce prickly ash seed follicles

Grind herbs to a powder using a coffee grinder, blender, or food chopper. Sprinkle on eggs, vegetables, meat, and fish for a spicy flavor.

Medicinal Benefits
Prickly ash bark has been used to treat rheumatic conditions, Raynaud's disease, and as a circulatory stimulant (Foster and Duke, 2003). Chewing on the bark results in a numbing effect on the gums. Prickly ash promotes the secretion of saliva and supports healthy gums. It is also antibacterial and anti-inflammatory.

Chemical Constituents
Prickly ash contains alkaloids, alkylamide, which produces a numbing effect, courmarins, resins, and tannins (Hoffman, 2003). The bark contains the alkaloid chelerythrine that has antibacterial and anti-inflammatory activity.

Growing Prickly Ash
Prickly ash can be grown from seed, but it has a low germination rate. They are also difficult to transplant. Scatter the seeds and hope for the best.

Safety Precautions
The root and bark may cause dermatitis (Duke, 2007). The spines on the trunk can cause puncture wounds.

Sustainability
Prickly ash is not common. When you locate a stand, look for branches that are hanging low that need to be pruned. If you come across seeds, scatter them in a similar area that the parent tree is growing. Prickly ash doesn't transplant well so avoid trying to dig one up and transplanting it to your yard or garden.

References
Duke, J. A. (2007). *Herb-A-Day*. Virginia Beach, VA: Eco Images.

Foster, S. and Duke. (2003). *Eastern/central medicinal plants and herbs*. New York, NY: Houghton Mifflin Co.

Hoffman, D. (2003). *Medical herbalism: The science and practice of herbal medicine*. Rochester, VT: Healing Arts Press.

PURSLANE
(Portulaca oleracea)
Purslane Family (Portulacaceae)

Description

Purslane is a naturalized summer green, one that doesn't emerge until later in the spring after the daytime temperatures climb into the eighties. Look for it in garden beds and edges of lawns where there is plenty of sunlight. Purslane is easy to identify. It has thick, succulent leaves and reddish-purple stems that sprawl across the ground and form clumps. It has adapted to growing in hot, sunny conditions by storing excess water in the leaves and stems, making it drought tolerant. Small, yellow flowers with five petals appear on bright, sunny mornings and are open for only a few hours before closing up. Following the flower is a seed capsule that releases numerous tiny black seeds.

Preparation and Uses

Leaves and stems are edible with a mild, somewhat tart taste. Stems are tender and crispy and make a nice addition to salads or as a cooked green with potatoes or other vegetables. They can also be preserved by pickling or tincturing with vinegar.

Purslane Pickles

Adds a tart, crunchy addition to your salad or vegetable dish.

- 1 pint purslane stems and leaves, washed and rinsed
- ¾ cup water
- ¾ cup apple cider vinegar
- 2 tablespoons field garlic or wild onions, chopped
- 2 teaspoons sea salt
- 1 tablespoon organic cane sugar

Pack the purslane in a pint jar. In a saucepan, combine the water, vinegar, garlic or onions, sea salt, and cane sugar. Bring to a boil. Pour the brine over the purslane, making sure to submerge all the purslane under the brine. Cover the jar and place in the refrigerator for at least 3 days before eating.

Nutritional Benefits

Purslane is nutritive and the best leafy source of omega-3 fatty acids (Duke, 1997). Omega-3 fatty acids are essential in preventing blood clots. The fresh greens contain calcium and magnesium in a one-to-one ratio, which makes it most protective for the heart. Purslane is also an excellent source of vitamins A, C, and E.

Constituents

Purslane contains carotenoids, omega 3 fatty acids, alkaloids, and oxalic acid. It also contains anti-inflammatory and vulnerary properties (Winston, 2016).

Growing Purslane

Purslane is easy to grow if you give it space. It likes hot, sunny conditions in disturbed soil and is a common volunteer in most gardens that haven't been sprayed with herbicides. Purslane is easily propagated from seed. It is also an annual and starts producing seed from mid to late summer. Collect the seeds and store overwinter in a brown paper bag. When the temperatures have climbed into the seventies, usually late May or early June, it's time to scatter the seeds where you want them to grow.

Safety Precautions

Avoid using with calcium oxalate kidney stones (Winston, 2016).

Poisonous Look-Alike

Spotted spurge (*Euphorbia* spp.) is another sprawling plant that grows in similar conditions as purslane. It also has reddish stems, but the leaves are much smaller and not as succulent. When the leaves and stems are broken, it exudes a white, milky sap that is toxic.

References

Duke, J. A. (1997). *The green pharmacy*. Emmaus, PA: Rodale Press.

Winston, D. (2016). "The worst weeds are your best medicine: The common and weedy plant material medica." Lecture notes from 2016 Medicines from the Earth.

RED CLOVER
(Trifolium pratense)
Pea Family (Fabaceae)

Description
Red clover is mainly a biennial, non-native species. It was introduced from Europe and is cultivated and planted as a cover crop to fix nitrogen in soil. It grows in a variety of conditions, including wet and dry meadows, open forests, and forest margins. Red clover is a low-growing herbaceous plant that reaches about two feet in height. Leaves are compound with three leaflets that are oval shaped with white chevrons on the upper surfaces. Pink, pea-like flowers develop in tight clusters above the upper leaves with five sepals and five petals. The fruit is a small, one-seeded pod.

Preparation and Uses
Red clover flowers have a wide variety of uses. It is best used as an extract or tea using fresh or dried flowers. The dried flower heads can be ground and used as flour.

Medicinal Benefits and Energetics
Red clover is nutritive, but it is also an alterative and supports lymphatic cleansing.

Chemical Constituents
Red clover contains genistein and daidzein and other isoflavones.

Growing Conditions
Red clover reproduces by seed. Collect the flower heads before they release their seeds and scatter them where you want them to grow.

Safety Precautions
Not for use during pregnancy or lactation (Gaia Herbs, 2021). When making tea from dried clover, avoid using brown plant material. This indicates oxidizing due to improper drying.

References
Gaia Herbs. (2021). "Red Clover." Retrieved from https://www.gaiaherbs.com/blogs/herbs/red-clover

REDBUD
(Cercis canadensis)
Pea Family (Fabaceae)

Description

When the redbud tree blooms, you know that spring has arrived. Its flowers appear in conjunction with the mating calls of songbirds and the chorus of frogs in the ponds and swamps. Redbud grows in the eastern part of the United States, from New Jersey to central Florida and west to Texas and Nebraska. To locate a redbud tree, look for pinkish purple or fuchsia-colored patches in the understory of the forest or its edges. It is one of the most attractive flowering trees in the forest.

As a member of the pea family, redbud has irregular-shaped pea-like flowers. The flowers grow in umbels along the branches and sometimes trunk of the tree before the leaves have come out. Pollinators such as bees, butterflies, and other insects are attracted to the flowers for their nectar.

Following the flowers are pods. While the pods are developing, distinctive heart-shaped leaves begin forming, partially hiding the flat pods. In the beginning the pods are greenish pink in color, becoming pink, and finally turning dark brown by the end of the summer.

Preparation and Uses

Redbud flowers and buds are edible and add bright colors as well as vitamin C to salads or dessert dishes. They are best picked while still in the greenish-pink phase, when they are between two to three inches in length. This is when they are the most tender. As the pods mature, they become tough and non-palatable. At this stage they can be stir-fried like snow peas. Remove the tough end points first.

Medicinal Benefits

Redbud flowers have a high vitamin C and vitamin A content.

Growing

Redbuds are easily grown from seed or from seedlings and will grow in full sun to part shade. Redbuds can tolerate a wide range of soil types.

SASSAFRAS
(Sassafras albidum)
Laurel Family (Lauraceae)

Description

Sassafras is a plant that most people have heard about, especially if you add root beer to the name. It grows as a small tree, often forming thickets by sending out roots underground. It has an extensive range, from Maine south to Florida and west to Texas, usually along the edges of forests where it gets plenty of sunlight. Sassafras is easily recognized in the summer by its mitten-shaped leaves. The bark of mature trees is deeply furrowed.

In late winter or early spring, yellowish-green clusters of flowers appear at the end of the stems before the leaves have developed. Sassafras is dioecious with male and female flowers on separate trees. The fruit is a blue-black single-seeded inedible berry that dangles from reddish stems.

By late summer, the leaves begin changing to a yellow-orange and deep red color before dropping to the ground in early autumn. Sassafras can be recognized in winter by the greenish bark and lighter-colored buds. Scratching the bark with your thumbnail and sniffing it will reveal a spicy aroma that is characteristic of sassafras. The sure test comes from digging up the root and smelling for the root beer flavor.

Parts Used

Roots, leaves, flowers

Filé Powder

Use as a thickener for gumbo or for soups and stews.

Look for sassafras in the spring when young leaves are developing. Snip off the leaves and hang to dry indoors out of sunlight. Once they are completely dry, strip the leaves and grind in a food processor or grinder. Store the powder in a glass jar away from direct light or heat. Add filé to liquids just before serving. Adding it while the liquid is boiling will yield a slimy, stringy texture.

Preparation and Uses

Sassafras buds start swelling in late winter and early spring. The flower buds are larger than the leaf buds. Flowers and leaf buds can be nibbled on while hiking or gathered and added to salads or vegetables for a spicy flavor. Young leaves are also spicy tasting and mucilaginous. Dried and powdered, they make a tasty seasoning and thickener for soups and stews. The root is the part used to make sassafras tea. Its pleasant flavor makes it a popular drink among foragers. Some use the bark of the root, but young roots can also be used, especially if they are coming up in an area where you don't want them. Sassafras oil is distilled from the root and can be used with other ingredients as a massage oil.

Sassafras Tea

Enjoy this beverage in the spring.

- 6–10 sassafras roots
- 1 quart cold water

Place roots in a pot and cover them with cold water. Bring to a boil, reduce heat, and continue to cook until the water has turned a deep red. Strain and serve. Sweeten to taste.

Medicinal Benefits and Energetics

Roots and root bark are warm, sweet, and pungent. Sassafras tea is used to thin the blood. It is a diaphoretic and used for fevers and flus (Wood, 2009).

Chemical Constituents

The root bark contains volatile oils (including safrole), lignans, and tannins (Wood, 2009).

Growing Sassafras

Even though sassafras spreads with underground rhizomes, sprouts taken from the rhizomes generally do not survive. Young seedlings that still have the primary root can be successfully planted. Once started, they will form a colony.

Safety Precautions

Safrole, a compound found in oil of sassafras, is reported to be a carcinogen and led to the ban of sassafras in root beer by the FDA. However, volatile oils are destroyed when heated. Regardless, drink in moderation.

References

Wood, M. (2009). *The earthwise herbal: A complete guide to new world medicinal plants.* Berkeley, CA: North Atlantic Books.

SELF-HEAL, HEAL-ALL
(Prunella vulgaris)
Mint Family (Lamiaceae)

Medicinal Benefits and Energetics
Self-heal is slightly bitter and pungent but mostly bland. It is a cooling herb and slightly moistening.

Parts Used
Dried flower, spike, and leaves

Uses
Aerial parts can be used raw in a salad or infused in hot water to make a tea or tincture.

Self-Heal Tea
A boost to the immune system while providing much needed nutrients.

- 1 quart water
- 4 teaspoons dried heal-all
- 5 teaspoon dried red clover flowers
- 3 teaspoons dried spearmint

Heat water to boiling. Pour over herbs and let steep for 1 hour. Strain and serve.

Constituents
Self-heal contains triterpenoid saponins, rutin, hyperoside, caffeic acid, d-camphor, and d-fenchone and is antibacterial, antimutagenic, diuretic, hypotensive agent, and vulnerary. It also contains antiviral properties and can be used for herpes simplex type I and II and shingles (Winston, 2016).

References
Winston, D. (2016). "The worst weeds are your best medicine: The common and weedy plant material medica." Lecture notes from 2016 Medicines from the Earth.

SERVICEBERRY
(*Amelanchier* spp.)
Rose Family (Rosaceae)

Description

Serviceberry is a small tree or shrub that grows in the understory of hardwood forests and along the shores of lakes, rivers, and streams. Drooping clusters of white flowers with five petals emerge early in the spring before the leaves have developed. Leaves are oval-shaped and toothed. The fruits are berries that ripen in May or June, depending on the area. The fruits have a size and appearance to blueberries except that they turn a deep reddish-purple when ripe.

Preparation and Uses

The fruits are edible and can be eaten raw or used in baking and to make jams and jellies. The fruits taste somewhat almond-like and add a nice flavor to cakes and cookies.

Growing Serviceberry

Serviceberry does best in part shade and well-drained soil. It requires little care.

SKULLCAP
(Scutellaria lateriflora)
Mint Family (Lamiaceae)

Description
Skullcap is a native perennial in the mint family with a characteristic square stem. It completely dies back in the winter and reemerges from the same root system the next spring. Leaves are toothed and in pairs. Its English and Latin name comes from the odd dish-shaped projection on the upper side of the calyx that disappears when the petals fall. At the leaf axils, a flower stalk develops with small lavender flowers facing one side.

Parts Used
Leaves, flowers, and roots

Preparation and Uses
The aerial parts of skullcap can be used fresh or dried as an infusion or a tincture.

Medicinal Benefits and Energetics
Skullcap is classified as a nervine tonic that affects the central nervous system and can be used as a hot infusion for nervous conditions, sleeplessness, bruxism (tooth-grinding), and other nervous disorders. It is a bitter and cooling herb and is often mixed with other relaxing herbs.

Constituents
Skullcap flavonoids baicalin and baicalein as well as the amino acids glutamine and GABA are thought to be the main constituents that may contribute to skullcap's anxiolytic properties (Awad et al., 2003). The leaves, stems, and roots contain the baicalin and baicalein flavonoids, but the greater concentrations have been determined to be in the roots. Skullcap also contains the flavonoids wogonin and scutellarin (Duke, 2011) as well as the iridoid catapol and volatile oils that are primarily sesquiterpenes (Eisenberg, 2012).

Growing Skullcap
Skullcap grows naturally in moist, swampy areas in much of the eastern United States and spreads with underground rhizomes like many mints. Skullcap can be divided or started from seeds in shade or part shade in rich soil. Water regularly.

Look-Alike
Skullcap has been mistaken for germander (*Teucrium canadense*), which is also in the mint family but has a square stem and flowers that are more pinkish.

References
Awad, R., Amason, J. T., Trudeau, V., Bergeron, C., Budzinski, J. W., Foster, B. C., Merali, Z. (2003). Phytochemical and biological analysis of skullcap (*Scutellaria lateriflora* L.): A medicinal plant with anxiolytic properties. *Phytomedicine, 10*(8), pp. 640–649.

Duke, J. A. (2011). "Plant rant: Dog days and mad-dog skullcaps." *The Green Farmacy Garden*. Retrieved from http://thegreenfarmacygarden .com/2011/09/06/plant-rant-dog-days-and -mad-dog-skullcaps.

Eisenberg, S. (2012). "Herbs for home use." Lecture, Tai Sopia.

Henson, S. (2007). Skullcap (*Scutellaria lateriflora*). HerbClip™ Online. Retrieved from http://cms.herbalgram.org/herbclip/337 /review44969.html.

SORREL
(Rumex acetosella, Oxalis spp.*)*
Buckwheat Family (Polygonaceae)
Wood Sorrel Family (Oxalidaceae)

Description

Sorrel is the common name refer-
ring to a number of different, unre-
lated plants. What they do share
is taste. Sorrel is derived from a
French word that means sour, and
both sheep sorrel and wood sorrel
taste sour when you bite into them.
Sheep sorrel is a common sorrel in yards and
gardens. It stands no more than twelve inches
tall and is available year-round. The leaves are
shaped like an arrowhead and are flared at the
base. In the spring it sends up a flower stalk with
spikes of yellowish-green to reddish-green flowers and seeds.

Wood Sorrel

Wood sorrel is the most common sorrel. Often
mistaken for clover, it has compound leaves
made up of three heart-shaped leaflets, joined at
their points to form a circle. Small yellow flowers
with five petals appear in the early spring and
continue into the summer on different plants.

Edible and Medicinal Uses

Leaves, flowers, and seeds are edible and can be
added raw to salads or added to cooked vegetables for a tart flavor. When eaten raw, they have
a cool, crisp taste. Sorrel is cooling and has been
used to reduce fevers and as a cooling agent.

Constituents

Oxalic acid contributes to the sour taste of sorrel.

Caution

Consuming oxalic acid in large quantities
absorbs calcium from the body and can be harmful. Those with kidney stones or who have had
kidney stones should avoid sorrels (AHPA's
Botanical Safety Handbook, 2013).

Growing Sorrels

Sorrels grow naturally in acidic soil and will
grow in shade or sun. Once started, they reseed
and colonize.

SPICEBUSH
(Lindera benzoin)
Laurel Family (Lauraceae)

Description
Spicebush is a shrub with smooth-edged oval-shaped aromatic leaves that grows along stream banks in moist woods. It sprouts tiny yellow flowers in the early spring before the leaves have emerged. Fruits develop in the summer, starting out green and then turning red as they ripen with a single seed in the center in early autumn.

Parts Used
Leaves, berries, bark, and twigs

Harvesting
Twigs can be gathered year-round to make tea.

Preparation and Uses
Spicebush twigs can be used to make a tea that is strengthening. The berries can be dried and ground and used as an allspice substitute.

Spicebush Twig Tea
An aromatic warming tea for the winter.

- 1 quart water
- 2 cups spicebush twigs, cut into 1–2-inch pieces
- 1 tablespoon maple syrup or other sweetener

Bring water to a boil. Add spicebush twigs and reduce heat. Simmer for 20 to 30 minutes. Strain and sweeten with maple syrup or other sweetener if desired.

Medicinal Benefits and Energetics
Spicebush has a somewhat sweet, pungent taste. It is warming and dry (Winston, 2016). The tea from the twigs can be used for colds, fever, and gas.

Chemical Constituents
Spicebush contains linderol, linderone, and linderalactone (Winston, 2016).

Growing Spicebush
Spicebush does best in moist, partially shaded conditions. It can be planted in your yard or garden but needs to be watered regularly the first year until it has fully established itself.

References
Winston, D. (2016). "The worst weeds are your best medicine: The common and weedy plant material medica." Lecture notes from 2016 Medicines from the Earth.

ST. JOHN'S WORT
(Hypericum punctatum)
St. John's wort Family (Hypericaceae)

Description
St. John's wort is a short-lived perennial wild-flower found in damp woods, thickets, and fields in the eastern part of the United States. Leaves are small with rounded tips and small, black dots on their surface. Flower stalks from one to three feet tall develop in late spring and early summer and produce clusters of small, yellow flowers with five petals, also with black dots. It is similar to *H. perforatum*, the European species, but has larger leaves and smaller flowers. St. John's wort reaches its peak flowering around the summer solstice and St. John's Day. For this reason, many believe that the best day to pick the St. John's wort flowers is on the feast of St. John on June 24.

Preparation and Uses
Flowers and leaf tops are harvested when the plant is in full bloom and can be used either in a tincture or infused in oil for salves and lotions.

Medicinal Benefits
St. John's wort is anti-inflammatory, astringent, vulnerary, nervine, and anti-microbial (Hoffman, 2003). The leaves and flowers are used in antiviral and antidepressant medications. Herbalists use the flowers for nerve pain and nerve damage. It is also used for melancholia and helps to bring light and joy into life (Winston and Maimes, 2007). According to Feather Jones, it is the perfect herb for the blues, sadness, and irritability (2014). It is also used to make lotions and salves for topical use.

Chemical Constituents
Leaves and flowers are a good source of hypericin, used in antiviral and antidepressant medications.

Growing Conditions
St. John's wort is easy to grow in shade or part sun as long as you water it regularly. It will produce more flowers and grow larger if it gets more light.

Safety Precautions
People with fair skin should avoid excessive exposure to sunlight when taking St. John's wort. It is also a detoxifier, so if you are taking pharmaceuticals you may want to avoid using St. John's wort (Duke, 2007).

Sustainability
The native St. John's wort is a short-lived perennial that may or may not come back in the same place each year. It helps to distribute the seeds in areas where you know they will grow.

References
Duke, J. A. (2007). *Herb-A-Day.* Virginia Beach, VA: Eco Images.

Hoffman, D. (2003). *Medical herbalism: The science and practice of herbal medicine.* Rochester, VT: Healing Arts Press.

Jones, F. (2014). "Herbs for cognitive therapy." American Herbalists Guild Symposium.

Winston, D. and Maimes, S. (2007). *Adaptogens: Herbs for strength, stamina, and stress relief.* Rochester, VT: Healing Arts Press.

Soothing Salve
A topical relief salve for shingles and herpes-related conditions as well as cuts and scrapes.

- 8 ounces lemon balm oil
- 4 ounces St. John's wort oil
- 2¼ ounces jojoba oil
- 4¼ ounces aloe water or aloe gel
- 1 tablespoon shea butter
- 1 ounce beeswax

Blend oils and aloe water or gel together in a double boiler. Add shea butter and beeswax. Heat on low heat until beeswax and shea butter have dissolved. Pour into containers and let cool. Use as needed.

SUMAC
(*Rhus* spp.)
Cashew Family (Anacardiaceae)

Description

Sumac is a native, deciduous shrub that grows on the sides of roads, interstates, and fields. It will grow anyplace where there is an opening of light or disturbed soil. It sends out horizontal underground stems that sprout and form colonies. There are about fifteen species  of sumac scattered throughout the United States. In the east, there are at least three species that are fairly common, all ripening at different times. Sumacs can be divided into two groups: poison sumac and non-poison sumac. The poison sumac (*Toxicodendron vernix*) has white berries that hang in loose clusters while the non-poison sumac (*Rhus* spp.) has red, tightly clustered berries. Large, compound leaves that turn flaming red in the fall are characteristic of both groups.

Staghorn Sumac (*Rhus typhina*)

Staghorn is the largest of the three eastern sumacs, reaching as high as thirty feet tall. The hairy twigs and leafstalks resemble the velvet on a deer's antlers. They begin blooming in mid-summer, with clusters of small, pinkish flowers. The flowers quickly develop into one-seeded fruits covered with bright red hairs.

Smooth Sumac (*Rhus glabra*)

Smooth sumac is a thicket shrub. It is similar to staghorn sumac but is smaller and has smooth twigs. The fruits are bright red and velvety and begin ripening in mid-summer, following the staghorn sumac.

Winged Sumac (*Rhus copallinum*)

About the time the staghorn sumac fruits finish ripening in late summer, the winged sumac starts blooming. Their flowers are more of a yellowish-green color. The smooth sumac (*Rhus glabra*) is similar to the staghorn but has smooth twigs and leafstalks. The fruits have more of a burgundy color when they ripen in the early fall.

Preparation and Uses

The secret to a good-tasting sumac drink is in the fruit. Quality fruits produce quality results. With sumac, it's watching for the right moment, when the fruits turn glowing, bright red, ideally before a rain. After a few days, they will lose that glow and start dulling in color. Breaking open a cluster will reveal hundreds of tiny insect eggs around the stems, maybe even a few caterpillars. It's best to get the fruits before they reach this stage. When ripe, the end branches should snap off easily.

All sumac species that bear red fruits can be used to make a tart, lemonade-like beverage. When berries are stripped from the branches, they can be infused in either hot or cold water. A cold-water infusion has a fruitier taste but must steep for a longer period of time. Cold water also extracts less of the astringent tannins than hot water.

Sumac can also be dried and ground into a reddish powder by placing the berries in a blender or coffee grinder. In some species, the powder can be siphoned off easily and used as a tart seasoning. In other species the seeds are so small that they sift through the strainer. In this case, the powder with the seeds can be used to make instant sumac-ade by infusing the powder in cold water (recipe on page 28). The longer it steeps, the stronger the flavor. Sumac-ade can also be used to make jellies, pies, or as a substitute for lemon juice.

Medicinal Benefits and Energetics

Sumac is sour and cooling. Sumac has antiseptic, astringent, and diuretic properties. It has a lemonade-like flavor and is a refreshing drink to have on a hot, summer afternoon. It strengthens the function of the kidneys and helps them to retain water. Sumac also helps with colds and flus, dripping sinuses, sore throat, and bronchitis (Wood, 2009).

Chemical Constituents

Fruits are covered with bright red hairs that are tart with citric acid and malic acid (Winston, 2016).

Growing Sumac

Sumac will grow almost anywhere. It will produce more fruits if it gets plenty of sunlight. Scatter the seed heads in the fall where you want them to grow. You can also put the berries out for the birds to eat and they will disperse the seeds through their droppings.

Safety Precautions

The poison sumac, which is fortunately a lot less common than the others, can cause a contact dermatitis reaction, similar to poison ivy. Poison sumac has white berries while the edible sumacs have red berries. Sumac is in the same family as poison ivy. Those who are allergic to poison ivy should use caution when using sumac for the first time.

References

Winston, D. (2016). "The worst weeds are your best medicine: The common and weedy plant material medica." Lecture notes from 2016 Medicines from the Earth.

Wood, M. (2009). *The earthwise herbal: A complete guide to new world medicinal plants*. Berkeley, CA: North Atlantic Books.

THISTLES
(*Cirsium* spp.)
Sunflower Family (Asteraceae)

Description

Thistles are usually biennial herbs with a fleshy taproot and a basal rosette of prickly leaves with teeth ending in sharp spines. The true thistles are in the genus *Cirsium* and include numerous species that are widespread across the country. Its flowers are typically shades of pink, lavender, purple, and yellow. Thistles grow in fields, edges of woods, fence lines, and other disturbed areas. Stems are covered with white wooly hairs.

Preparation and Uses

The first-year root is edible before the flower stalk develops. The flower stalk can be harvested before the flower has opened. Just cut the stalk at the base, remove the head, then peel off the fuzzy outer layer. The peeled stalk is similar to celery and can be used the same way. Thistle flowers can be chewed as a thirst quencher and to extract their nectar. A tea can be made from the flower buds.

Thistle Tincture

A combination of vinegar and brandy makes this tincture exceptionally tasty.

- 15–20 thistle stalks, peeled
- 2 cups balsamic vinegar
- 1½ cups wild cherry brandy
- ½ cup black raspberry liqueur

Fill a quart jar with thistle stalks. Cover with vinegar, brandy, and raspberry liqueur. Store in a dark pantry for at least 2 weeks. Thistle stalks can be added to salads. Tincture can be added to sparkling water.

Medicinal Benefits

Thistles are liver cleansers. They are also anti-inflammatory, astringent, and cooling.

Chemical Constituents

Thistles contain sesquiterpenes, compounds with anti-inflammatory and antibacterial properties (Winston, 2016). They are also high in minerals including magnesium, copper, calcium, iron, phosphorus, and more.

Growing Thistles

Thistles can be grown easily from seed. For an autumn germination, in late summer sow directly into the soil or scatter in the area you want them to grow. Thistles grow best in disturbed soil with average moisture.

Safety Precautions

Thistle leaves have sharp, dagger-like spines that can puncture. Strong gloves should be worn when harvesting thistles.

Sustainability

Thistles are in significant decline. Loss of habitat, herbicide spraying, and the release of non-native insects to control non-native thistle species are a threat to our thistles. Collect seeds when you can and either grow them or scatter them in areas where they will be allowed to grow.

References

Winston, D. (2016). "The worst weeds are your best medicine: The common and weedy plant material medica." Lecture notes from 2016 Medicines from the Earth.

USNEA LICHEN
(*Usnea* spp.)
Parmeliacaea Family

Lichens
Lichens are a combination of a fungus and an alga. Lichens are decomposers that come in all shapes and colors, including red, yellow, green, blue, and brown. Some hang from branches in long strands, while others have a leaf-like shape and cling to dead trees or rocks. Some grow on the trunks of trees, while others simply sit on top of the ground. They are very abundant and can be found throughout the world.

One thing they all have in common is their composition. They are all made up of two organisms living together in a symbiotic relationship. The fungus absorbs water and provides structure and protection for the algal cells that live wrapped up in the strands of the fungus mycelium. The algae contain chlorophyll and use it to convert sunlight into food sugars for both organisms through photosynthesis. Together they act as a new single entity, with reproductive structures and chemicals that differ from either of the original organisms. Plus, they receive minerals from rainwater and from the rocks, trees, soil, and other surfaces on which they grow.

Description
Usnea is a fruticose lichen and grows worldwide on the bark of trees, usually conifers, but can also be found on oak, hickory, walnut, and apple trees. It is pale grayish green in color and looks like tufts of hair. There are many species of usnea, all characterized by a stretchy internal "filament" or stem. One can take a strand of the pale grayish green lichen and pull away at the outer coating (cortex) to reveal a whiteish, elastic cord. It is the only lichen with a white core. Occasionally, they are covered with a grayish-colored lichen, referred to as old man's beard, otherwise known as usnea. This is the time to

harvest usnea and either dry it, prepare a tincture, or infuse in oil. It contains usnic acid, which has demonstrated antibacterial activity (Hoffman, 2003).

Harvesting Usnea
When winter storms and strong winds prune old trees, dropping their branches to the ground, this is a good time to look for usnea. It hangs in gray-green strands from the branches of trees in forests and the edges of swamps. When collecting usnea, it is best to only gather what has fallen to the forest floor, rather than taking it straight from the tree itself. This is because lichens grow very slowly. When you are out walking in the woods where usnea grows, keep an eye out for usnea on fallen branches and gather from there. Usnea has been referred to as the lungs of the forest and only grows in clean air, so when you are harvesting usnea, take a deep breath of fresh air because the air is pure.

Preparation and Uses
Usnea is more of a medicine than a food, although you can eat it or make a tea with it. The best way to use usnea is to make a tincture. Grind the herb to a powder in a grinder or with a pestle before tincturing. The immune boosting polysaccharides are best extracted using heat. There are other compounds that are not water-soluble that need alcohol for optimum benefits (Buhner, 2012). Usnea needs heat and alcohol for best results. Heat the herb first in the water with two parts water to one part herb. Heat just to the point of boiling and reduce heat. Continue to cook on low heat to half the water content. Let cool. Add an equal amount of grain alcohol as water to the mix. Cover and let steep for two weeks.

Medicinal Benefits and Energetics
Usnea is cooling with a slightly bitter taste. It is an immune system tonic that can be used in acute situations as well as for long-term immune enhancement and general prevention. Usnic acid is obtained from *Usnea* and is the most common source of antibiotic and antifungal lichen acids

(Hobbs, 1986). According to Ryan Drum (2021), it is among the best herbal antibiotics and protects against Streptococci and Staphylococci.

Chemical Constituents

Usnic acid is obtained from *Usnea* spp. and is "the most common source of antibiotic and antifungal lichen acids. (Hobbs, 1986). It is also immune modulating, astringent, and anti-inflammatory (de la Foret, 2020).

Sustainability

Usnea is slow growing and can easily be over-harvested. When harvesting usnea, look for freshly fallen branches.

References

Buhner, S. H. (2012). *Herbal antibiotics: Natural alternatives for treating drug-resistant bacteria.* North Adams, MA: Storey Publishing.

de la Foret, R. (2020). "Usnea." Rosalee de la Forêt." *Herbs with Rosalee.* Retrieved from https://www.herbalremediesadvice.org/usnea-herb.html.

Drum, R. (2021). "Wildcrafting medicinal plants." Retrieved from http://www.ryandrum.com/wildcrafting.htm.

Hobbs, C. (1986). *Usnea: Herbal Antibiotics.* Capitola, CA: Botanica Press.

Hoffman, D. (2003). *Medical herbalism: The science and practice of herbal medicine.* Rochester, VT: Healing Arts Press.

VIOLET
(Viola spp.)
Violet Family (Violaceae)

Description
Violets are perennial wildflowers that are found throughout the country and are easy to recognize with their heart-shaped leaves and irregular flowers. They are related to the cultivated pansies and Johnny-jump-ups. There are some fifty species of violets with flowers ranging from typical violet blue to yellow and white. Most species die back in the winter and reemerge the next spring from the same roots, but a few are evergreen and retain edible leaves all year. Violets grow just about everywhere, including lawns and meadows, in both dry and moist woods, fields, swamps, bogs, and along stream banks.

Preparation and Uses
Young violet leaves and flowers can be used for food and medicine. The blossoms are rich in vitamin C and the leaves are rich in vitamins A and C as well as iron. Violet leaves and flowers can be used raw in salads or herbal vinegars. As a tea they can be used to relieve dryness and for dry coughs (de la Foret, 2020).

Medicinal Benefits and Energetics
Violets are cooling and moistening. They act as an alterative and a demulcent. Leaves can be infused in oil and made into a salve to relieve hot and dry skin conditions. Violet flowers contain a significant amount of rutin, which strengthens capillary blood vessels, reduces cholesterol, and prevents blood clots (de la Foret, 2020).

Growing Violets
If you have a partially shaded or shady area in your yard, you probably already have violets. They are easily transplanted or started from seed. Once established, they require very little care.

Safety Precautions
The halberd-leaf violet (*V. hastata*) with yellow flowers may cause vomiting.

References
de la Foret, R. (2020). *Wild remedies*. Carlsbad, CA: Hay House, Inc.

WAX MYRTLE
(Morella cerifera)
Wax Myrtle Family (Myricaceae)

Description and Habitat
Wax myrtle is an evergreen shrub that grows in moist soil along banks of marshes, swamps, forests, and sand dunes. Its leaves have toothed edges beyond the middle and are lance-shaped with yellow resinous dots on the underside that release a scent when crushed. The flowers are small, green or yellow in color, and develop in a narrow, cylindrical cluster at the base of the leaf in early spring. They are followed by a cluster of one-seeded bluish-white fruits that mature in the fall.

Parts Used
Leaves, bark

Preparation and Uses
Wax myrtle leaves can be used fresh or dried to make a tea and as an insect repellent, either as an oil infusion or a tincture to use as a spray. Younger leaves in the spring are not as bitter as older leaves. The bark can be used as a tea or tincture.

Medicinal Benefits and Energetics
Wax myrtle is astringent and pungent and can be used for diarrhea, dysentery, and catarrh (Foster and Duke, 2000). A tea from the leaves helps with fevers, headache, and stomachache (Moerman, 1998).

Chemical Constituents
Wax myrtle contains triterpenes, flavonoids, tannins, resins, and gums.

Growing Conditions
Wax myrtle grows along the coast at the edges of freshwater or slightly brackish marshes, swamps, and in moist, sandy soil. Seeds germinate easily and grow quickly.

References
Foster, S. and Duke. (2003). *Eastern/central medicinal plants and herbs*. New York, NY: Houghton Mifflin Co.

Moerman, Dan. "Native American Ethnobotany Database." http://www.umd.umich.edu/cgi-bin/herb.

Wax Myrtle Tea
An astringent tea that helps with congestion and stimulates circulation.

- 1 cup hot water
- 10 wax myrtle leaves
- 1 tablespoon honey or to taste

Pour hot water over wax myrtle leaves. Cover and let steep about 5 to 10 minutes. Strain and sweeten to taste.

WILD BEANS
(Strophostyles helvola, S. umbellata)
Pea Family (Fabaceae)

Description

Wild bean is a native annual that is the ancestor of our cultivated garden green bean and looks very similar. It germinates in the spring and develops compound leaves with three oval-shaped leaflets and mostly smooth margins. The vine grows all summer and climbs over everything in its path. By the end of summer, it starts developing irregular, pea-shaped flowers that are pinkish purple followed by a pod that looks very much like a cultivated green bean with a tougher shell and smaller seeds. It can be used the same way as a green bean.

Uses

Young beans can be harvested while they are still tender before the seeds have developed. Just break off the ends and bring to a boil for about 20 minutes. Use as you would a green bean. When the pods have filled out, the shells are too tough to eat, so place them in a pan of salted water, bring to a boil for about 20 minutes, cool, and shell like a shelled bean.

Caution

Avoid eating raw beans. They contain lectins that might cause digestive discomfort.

WILD BLACK CHERRY
(*Prunus serotina*)
Rose Family (Rosaceae)

Description

Wild black cherry is a native medium-sized tree that occurs over most of the eastern half of the United States. The leaves are elliptical, finely toothed, dark green above, and lighter  beneath. Small, white, aromatic flowers with five petals hang in drooping racemes in mid-spring. Following the flowers are small, almost black fruits with a single seed in the center. Black cherry fruits begin ripening in July in southern areas and August on higher elevations and farther north. The twigs are reddish-brown and, when scratched, emit a strong, pungent odor. Its twigs and bark contain lenticels, tiny pores that provide openings for gas exchange.

Parts Used
Inner bark, fruit

Preparation and Uses
Fruits are sweet and juicy and can be eaten raw off the tree for a thirst quencher or made into a juice that is blood-building and strengthening. Fall is the time to harvest the bark. Choose young saplings and strip off the outer bark. Carefully dry the bark in the shade and store in an air-tight container away from light.

Cocoa Cherry Puffs
A blend of wild cherries and cocoa to give that burst of energy when needed.

- 2 cups unbleached white flour
- ⅔ cup organic cocoa powder
- ⅔ cup butter, softened
- 1 cup raw, organic sugar
- 2 eggs
- 2 cups wild black cherry (*Prunus serotina*) pulp
- 1 vanilla bean, halved lengthwise and scraped
- 4 ounces organic cacao nibs

Preheat oven to 350°F. Mix flour and cocoa powder in a large bowl and set aside. In a separate bowl, blend softened butter and sugar. Add in eggs and wild black cherry pulp and mix. Combine with flour mixture and add vanilla bean and cacao nibs. Blend well. Drop by teaspoons onto oiled baking dish. Bake at 350°F for 8 to 10 minutes or until done.

Medicinal Benefits
Scratching the bark of wild cherry releases a scent that is the odor of benzaldehyde. Wild cherry bark is antitussive, expectorant, astringent, nervine, and antispasmodic (Hoffman, 2003). The taste is bitter. A tincture from the bark suppresses coughing and is used to treat asthma, bronchitis, and other respiratory conditions (Wood, 2009). Wild cherry bark has been used traditionally for coughs, fevers, colds, sore throats, lung ailments, bronchitis, pneumonia, and other ailments (Foster and Duke, 2003).

Chemical Constituents
Bark, leaves, and seeds contain a cyanogenic glycoside, prunasin, which is converted to hydrocyanic acid (HCN) as it decomposes (Hoffman, 2003). It also contains benzaldehyde and tannins (Mills, 1991).

Growing Black Cherries

Black cherries are easy to grow. They volunteer in yards, gardens, and fields where birds drop their seeds. Give them a place and let them grow.

Safety Precautions

Large doses of black cherry bark can be toxic. Cattle have been poisoned from eating wilted foliage of wild cherry trees and children have been poisoned from eating too many cherry pits. Large doses of wild cherry bark can be toxic.

References

Foster, S. and Duke. (2003). *Eastern/central medicinal plants and herbs.* New York, NY: Houghton Mifflin Co.

Hoffman, D. (2003). *Medical herbalism: The science and practice of herbal medicine.* Rochester, VT: Healing Arts Press.

Mills, S. Y. 1991. *Out of the earth: The essential book of herbal medicine.* London, England: Viking Arkana.

Wood, M. (2009). *The earthwise herbal: A complete guide to new world medicinal plants.* Berkeley, CA: North Atlantic Books.

WILD GRAPES
(*Vitis* spp.)
Grape Family (Vitaceae)

Description

Wild grapes are easily recognized by their woody
vines that climb high into
trees, often at the edges of
woods. There are at least
two dozen species of wild
grapes that occur in the
United States. Flowers are a greenish-white and
appear in the spring and are mildly fragrant.
Fruits develop later in the summer and mature
in late summer or early fall and turn purplish
black when ripe.

Muscadine Grapes *(Vitis rotundifolia)*

Muscadine grapes are the ancestor of cultivated
grapes in the south and grow from Delaware
south to central Florida. They are cultivated
as far west as Texas and northward along the
Mississippi River to Missouri in woods, thickets,
sand dunes, and swamps. It is a vigorous, high-
climbing deciduous vine with tendrils that may
grow up to one hundred feet in the wild.

Muscadine leaves are somewhat heart-
shaped with a V-shape at the base with deeply
serrated margins. It has small, greenish flowers
in the spring, followed by fruits that ripen in late
summer and early fall about the time the leaves
start changing color. Grapes turn dark purple to
black when ripe.

The scuppernong is a sub-species of the
muscadine and also grows wild. It is sometimes
referred to as the blond muscadine. They are
lighter in color and have a thinner skin than the
purple ones.

Fox Grapes *(Vitis labusca)*

Fox grapes are native to eastern North American
and are the ancestors of a number of grape cultivars. Its leaves are four to six inches long and
vary in shape but generally have three lobes.
Yellowish-green flowers appear in June and give
way to drooping clusters of blue-black fruits. The
taste is foxy and earthy.

Parts Used

Fruits, leaves

Harvesting Wild Grapes

Grapes begin ripening late summer into the fall.
They can be gathered rather quickly by holding
a bucket under the clusters and picking or clip-
ping them by the handful, letting them drop into
the bucket as they fall.

Preparation and Uses

Young grape leaves are edible but bitter and
dry. They can be added to salads or cooked with
greens. Larger leaves can be used as a wrap.
All grapes are edible, but most wild grapes are
small and acidic with very little juice. Muscadine
grapes, however, are sweet to eat straight from
the vine and make excellent jelly, pies, and wine.

Wild grapes contain lots of natural pectin
and can be used for making jelly without pur-
chasing commercial pectin. When making jelly,
be sure to use a few unripe ones since unripe
grapes have more pectin than ripe ones. You
may need to add extra sugar to get it to gel,
depending on your desired thickness. To make
grape juice, cover the grapes with water and boil
gently for about 10 minutes. Pour through a sieve
or food mill to remove the seeds. The resulting
juice can be sweetened and drunk as is or made
into jelly or jam. To make muscadine grape pies,
it is best to use the skins whole. Remove them
by squeezing the pulp into a bowl separate from
the skins. Place the pulp in a saucepan and heat
gently for about 5 minutes, then pour through a
food mill to remove the seeds. Combine the pulp
with the skins.

Muscadine Preserves

A sweet and sour preserve to spread on hot biscuits.

- 2 cups muscadine grapes, hulled and seeds removed
- 1 cup organic cane sugar

Place grapes and sugar in saucepan and bring to a gentle boil. Reduce heat and cook on medium for 25 minutes, stirring frequently or until thickened. Pour into sterilized jars and seal.

Muscadine Shrub

Add sparkling water and drink as a cooling summer drink.

- 2 cups muscadine preserves
- 2 cups organic balsamic vinegar

Place preserves in a quart jar. Add balsamic vinegar. Mix well. Store in a cool, dark pantry for at least 2 weeks.

Health Benefits

Muscadine grapes have sweet pulp but a sour skin. Its leaves are bitter and astringent. Muscadine grapes are among the richest sources of antioxidants, especially ellagic acid and resveratrol (M.D. News, 2008).

Chemical Constituents

Muscadine grapes are among the richest sources of antioxidants, especially ellagic acid and resveratrol. A puree of skins and pulp was found to be an excellent source of resveratrol, dietary fiber, essential minerals, high in carbohydrates, and low in fat and protein (Stanley, 1997). According to Jim Duke (2007), grape leaves are the best source of resveratrol, and he believes the wild ones to have more than the tame ones. The resveratrol is one of those compounds that protects the plant from their natural enemies.

Growing Grapes

Wild grapes are easy to grow and require little maintenance. They will produce more fruit if they get light.

Look-Alike

Moonseed (*Menispermum canadense*) fruits resemble grapes, but the vine lacks tendrils, and the fruit contains a single crescent-shaped seed in the center that is poisonous. Virginia creeper (*Parthenocissus quinquefolia*) and peppervine (*Ampelopsis arborea*) have blue-black berries that may resemble grapes but the leaves of Virginia creeper are divided into five leaflets and the peppervine has paired leaflets.

References

Duke, J. A. (2007). *Herb-A-Day*. Virginia Beach, VA: Eco Images.

M.D. News. Special Feature. (2008). "The health benefits of grapes, wines and nutraceuticals." Retrieved from https://www.cypressbend vineyards.com/media/1269/md-news-june -2008.pdf.

Stanley, D. (November 20, 1997). "Muscadine grapes: A new health food and an alternative crop." Retrieved from https://www.ars.usda. gov/news-events/news/research-news/1997 /muscadine-grapes-a-new-health-food-and -an-alternative-crop/.

WILD LETTUCE
(*Lactuca canadensis*)
Sunflower Family (Asteraceae)

Description
Wild lettuce is a native that grows in the eastern and central parts of the United States. It is a biennial that emerges in the spring and grows through the summer and into the fall and winter. Young leaves are deeply lobed and look very much like dandelion leaves when they first emerge, but dandelion leaves are a dark green above and below, while wild lettuce leaves are a light color underneath. A milky sap exudes from the stem when a leaf is picked. The next spring, wild lettuce sends up a flower stalk that may reach ten feet tall, and numerous small, dandelion-like yellow flowers with five petals develop at the tips of the upper branches.

Uses
As a food, the leaves when very young can be used raw in a salad or cooked as a green. The flowers, leaves, and stalks can be tinctured and used as a sedative and pain reliever.

Health Benefits
Wild lettuce is a bitter herb and is used as a nervine, anodyne, and antispasmodic. As an antispasmodic it can be used for whooping cough and dry, irritated coughs (Hoffman, 2003).

Constituents
Wild lettuce contains lactucin, flavonoids, and coumarin (Hoffman, 2003).

Safety Precautions
Use only the young leaves for food and in moderation. The latex that develops in older leaves may cause dizziness or nausea.

References
Hoffman, D. (2003). *Medical herbalism: The science and practice of herbal medicine.* Rochester, VT: Healing Arts Press.

WILD MUSTARDS
(Alliaria petiolata, Barbarea **spp.** *Brassica* **spp.,** *Capsella bursa-pastoris,*
Cardamine **spp.,** *Lepidium virginicum)*
Mustard Family (Brassicaceae)

Description

The mustard family is quite large with more than four thousand species worldwide. Many of these plants were brought to the United States and have been cultivated to produce vegetables that most people are familiar with, including broccoli, kale, and cabbage. All mustards have four-petaled flowers with six stamens and a single pistil in the center. The color varies from white and yellow to pink and purple. Seedpods also come in many shapes and sizes. The taste varies among the individual species, but they all share that spicy, pungent taste (Elpel, 2006).

Bittercress *(Cardamine hirsuta, C. pensylvanica)*

Bittercress is a low-growing annual that emerges in the fall, grows through the winter, and produces small white flowers in the spring. Its leaves and flowers have a horseradish-like flavor and can be added raw to salads or preserved in vinegar.

Garlic Mustard *(Alliaria petiolata)*

Garlic mustard is a low-growing winter annual that sprouts in the fall or spring and forms clusters of nearly circular leaves with rounded teeth. They produce flower stalks in the spring that grow two to three feet topped by small florets of buds that open into small white flowers. The flowers are followed by slender, green seed pods that turn dark when mature.

Garlic mustard is on the invasive species list and is even banned from planting in some areas. Instead of planting garlic mustard, find an area where it is already established and remove it. As Jim Duke often said, "If you want to get rid of something, find a use for it." And with garlic mustard, it is food medicine. It contains isothiocyanates, one of the cancer preventives of the mustard family and allyl sulfides that are cancer preventives of garlic (Duke, 1992). Harvest the seed stalk before it releases its seed and hang it in a paper bag. As the pods dry, the seedpods

will open and release the seed that can be dried and ground as a mustard seed. This also prevents the plant from spreading its seed.

Caution

Only eat garlic mustard leaves if you crush the leaf and make sure it has a garlic-like smell. *Senecio* spp. has leaves that could be confused with garlic mustard and are toxic.

Peppergrass *(Lepidium virginicum)*

Peppergrass is a common weed that grows in waste places and disturbed soils throughout the United States from Canada to Central America. Not a grass at all, peppergrass is an annual that germinates in the fall or spring and develops a basal rosette of leaves. The leaves are small and narrow and blend in with other plants or hide beneath those that have died back for the winter. It develops a flower stalk soon after germinating that reaches up to two feet tall with single leaves that are slightly toothed and alternate on the stem. At the top of the stalk are rounded clusters of tiny, white flowers with four petals. The fruit is a tiny, almost round, flat seedpod with a slight notch at the apex. The seedpods are so numerous that it makes them easy to spot.

Shepherd's Purse *(Capsella bursa-pastoris)*

A low-growing inconspicuous annual, it is usually not noticed until it produces seedpods. A basal rosette develops during the winter months with deeply lobed, toothed leaves. The flower stalk is about a foot tall and is topped with small white flowers with four petals. The flat pods are triangular and notched at the tip, giving it the appearance of a heart. Shepherd's purse contains calcium, phosphorus, potassium, ascorbic acid, beta-carotene, tocopherol, and choline (Duke, 2007).

Toothwort (*Cardamine* spp.)

Toothwort, also referred to as crinkleroot or pepperroot is a native perennial that grows in the shade of the forest. It only makes an appearance during the winter months and forms a mat across the forest floor with leaves that are divided into leaflets with prominent white veins. The root is a white, horizontal rhizome that spreads just above the ground. This is the part most frequently used. It has a horseradish-like taste and can be used in the same way as horseradish.

Watercress (*Nasturtium officinale*)

Watercress grows in and along the edges of slow-moving streams. It is made up of leaflets arranged in pairs on a common stalk with a larger single leaf at the tip. Its flowers have four white petals.

Winter cress; Yellow Rocket (*Barbarea vulgaris, B. verna*)

Ancestors of our cultivated mustards, both winter cress and yellow rocket have dark green, glossy leaves that are deeply lobed. Also referred to as creasy greens, these are some of the first greens harvested in the spring. The leaves resemble those of watercress but are darker, shiny, and have smaller leaflets.

The cresses can be annuals, biennials, or rarely perennials. They generally like the cool weather and grow through the winter. As soon as the days start warming up, the cresses bolt, bloom, and go to seed. Flowers of both species are small and yellow, and the fruit is a four-angled or rounded green pod (Duke, 1992).

Nutritional Benefits

All mustards are edible. The greens are outstanding sources of vitamins A, B1, B2, and C, as well as many trace minerals and fibers. The flower buds are equally rich in vitamins and minerals and have the additional advantage of being high in protein.

Some mustard species taste better than others. During the winter, when most plants are dormant, the young basal leaves of various mustard species can be harvested and added to salads or cooked as a potherb.

The seedpods, while young and tender, can be added to salads and steamed vegetables. Collect the whole seed stalk as the pods are just beginning to split open and spread on mats to dry for a few days, then thresh them to release the seed. The dried seeds can be ground and used in any recipe calling for dry mustard. They can also be crushed and mixed with vinegar or oil for a dressing or marinade.

Medicinal Benefits and Energetics

A common characteristic among members of the mustard family is pungency. Most are hot, spicy, warming, and bitter, which can stimulate the appetite and digestion. Mustards are also drying. Poultices from mustard seeds are used to break up mucus congestion (Pengelly, 2004).

Chemical Constituents

The spicy, pungent taste can be attributed to glycosides. Mustard oil glycosides are known as glucosinolates and are compounds found in the mustard family. They are mainly in the seeds but also occur in the leaves and roots. Mustard seeds also contain mucilage and essential fatty acid (Pengelly, 2004).

Growing Mustards

If you have a garden that hasn't been sprayed with herbicides, the chances are pretty good you already have some mustards growing. Allow last year's garden beds to grow and wait for the plants to flower for identification purposes before removing them. If you don't have them, look for seeds in fields, edges of woods, and organic gardens. These can be dispersed in late summer or early autumn since this is when they normally germinate.

Uses

All parts are edible. Leaves can be added to salads, soups, and other cooked vegetables for a pleasantly pungent flavor. The seeds can be tossed into a salad or added to oil and vinegar to make a spicy salad dressing.

Safety Precautions

Be aware of the environment in which you are harvesting. Find out what the water quality is like. If you're not sure, use the watercress only in cooked dishes. Cooking it will destroy most harmful organisms.

References

Duke, J. A. (1992). *Handbook of edible weeds.* Boca Raton: CRC Press.

Duke, J. A. (2007). *Herb-A-Day.* Virginia Beach, VA: Eco Images.

Elpel, T. (2006). *Botany in a day: The patterns method of plant identification.* Pony, MT: HOPS Press, LLC.

Hoffman, D. (2003). *Medical herbalism: The science and practice of herbal medicine.* Rochester, VT: Healing Arts Press.

Pengelly, A. (2004). *The constituents of medicinal plants.* Cambridge, MA: CABI Publishing.

WILD ROSE
(*Rosa* spp.)
Rosaceae

Description

Roses are uplifting and a symbol of love and beauty. They can help soothe a broken heart, anger, or grief. Roses are branching shrubs armed with stout, hooked thorns on branches and stems. There are more than five hundred species of rose that grow in a variety of habitats and environments. The wild roses generally have a stronger scent than cultivated varieties. Leaves are compound with five- to seven-toothed leaflets. It blooms in late spring with fragrant pink or white flowers that have five petals and yellow center stamens. The fruit is a hip and turns red when it ripens in late fall.

Parts Used

Petals, flower buds, and fruits

Rose Water Spritzer
A cooling, refreshing facial mist or body spray.

- 7 tablespoons rose water
- 1 tablespoon witch hazel extract
- 10 drops lavender essential oil

Combine ingredients and add to a 4-ounce spritzer bottle. Use as a topical spray for a refreshing feeling.

Preparation and Uses

Wild roses are wonderfully fragrant. Rose petals and buds can be infused in hot or cold water to make rose water, in alcohol to make a tincture, or in oil to make lotions and salves. Rose petals can also be covered with honey in a glass jar to make rose petal honey. Just cover and store the glass jar in a cool, dark place for two weeks, then strain and use as a sweetener. Rose petals and fruits can be used to make tea, jelly, syrup, or preserves. To use rose hips, cut off the end with a knife, cut the fruit in half, and remove the fibrous seeds.

Medicinal Benefits and Energetics

Roses are cooling and drying. They are also anti-inflammatory and a relaxing nervine. Rose hips are one of the best botanical sources of vitamin C and can be used for colds and flu and to boost the immune system. They are also a mild laxative and a diuretic.

Chemical Constituents

Rose hips contain vitamin E, selenium, manganese, and the B-complex vitamins as well as magnesium, potassium, sulfur, and silicon.

Growing Roses

When growing wild roses, check to see which roses are native to your area. Once planted, they require little care other than to prevent other plants from crowding them out before they get established.

Safety Precautions

Allergies to rose hips have been reported (AHPA's Botanical Safety Handbook, 2013).

YARROW
(Achillea millefolium)
Sunflower Family (Asteraceae)

Description
Yarrow was at one time considered non-native, an invasive alien, and eliminated from the landscape. Then, it was determined that it was native, and it was okay to keep it. Its medicinal virtues have since surfaced and it has now become one to grow and include in the herbal medicine chest. Yarrow is a native perennial with finely divided aromatic leaves and small, white, sometimes pink flowers that form a flat-topped cluster at the top of a gray-green, leafy stem. There are numerous cultivars with different colored flowers but lacking the medicinal value of the native yarrow.

Parts Used
Aerial parts, leaves, and flowers

Preparation and Uses
Yarrow is a wound healer. Fresh leaves and flowers can be used as a poultice on cuts and wounds to stop bleeding. Yarrow can also be infused in oil for salve preparations for skin inflammation and wounds. Leaves and flowers can be used fresh or dried as a tea to promote sweating for lowering a fever or as a bitter tonic for digestion.

Medicinal Benefits and Energetics
Yarrow is astringent, drying, cooling, antibacterial, anti-inflammatory, and a diuretic. As a diaphoretic, it stimulates sweating and is good for lowering a fever.

Chemical Constituents
Yarrow contains essential oils of linalool, camphor, borneol, eucalyptol, flavonoids, alkaloids, tannins, and coumarins (Kuhn and Winston, 2008).

Growing Yarrow
Yarrow grows naturally in sunny fields and disturbed areas and transplants easily. It comes up easily from seeds and forms colonies.

Safety Precautions
Contact dermatitis is rare but possible. Avoid high doses if lactating. Avoid during pregnancy.

References
Kuhn, M. A., and Winston, D. (2008). *Herbal therapy & supplements: A scientific and traditional approach.* Philadelphia, PA: Wolters Kluwer/ Lippincott Williams & Wilkins.

YAUPON
(Ilex vomitoria)
Holly Family (Aquifoliaceae)

Description
Yaupon is a large evergreen shrub or small tree, often forming thickets along the Atlantic coast from Virginia south to central Florida and along the Gulf coast to southern Texas. It grows in dry, sandy soil near the ocean and can withstand strong winds and salty air. Its hardiness may account for its widespread use in landscaping in those areas where most plants would not survive. Its leaves are simple, alternate, and a glossy green with rounded teeth. Hollies have male and female flowers that bloom in the spring with numerous tiny white fragrant flowers. The berries mature in autumn and turn shiny red by winter, often remaining attached throughout the winter, making Yaupon popular for Christmas decorations.

Preparation and Uses
Yaupon is the only holly in North America known to contain caffeine. The leaves have to be roasted before the caffeine is soluble in water. Once they are roasted, they can be ground and steeped in hot water for a stimulating tea.

Yaupon with Turmeric and Cocoa Powder

A stimulating way to start the day.

- 2 cups boiling water
- 2 tablespoons roasted yaupon leaves
- 1 teaspoon turmeric powder
- 1 teaspoon cocoa powder
- 1 teaspoon maple syrup

Pour boiling water over yaupon leaves, cover, and let steep for 10 to 15 minutes. Add remaining ingredients and stir. Serve hot.

Chemical Constituents
Theobromine, theophylline, and caffeine are methylated xanthine alkaloids that occur in the leaves of yaupon. It also contains high concentrations of antioxidants that include chlorogenic acid, coumaric acid, and several flavonoids (Shufer, 2016).

Medicinal Benefits
Methylated xanthine alkaloids stimulate the central nervous system, enhancing alertness and warding off drowsiness.

Growing
Yaupon can be grown successfully in southern climates where the winters are fairly mild. Horticulturists and landscape gardeners use them in hedges and foundation plantings.

Safety Precautions
The berries are considered toxic and emetic.

Sustainability
Loss of habitat is the biggest threat. Seeds are dispersed by birds and will germinate wherever the conditions are right.

References
Shufer, V. (2016). "Yaupon holly: A North American plant source of caffeine." *Herbalgram*, February–April, 2016, No. 109.

YELLOW DOCK
(Rumex crispus)
Buckwheat Family (Polygonaceae)

Description
Yellow dock is a common weed found throughout the country. It is a perennial herb with dark green, lanceolate-shaped leaves with wavy margins. The older leaves often have scattered red splotches. The upper leaves that grow on the seed stalk are smaller and less numerous. The leaves on the young plant are basal, all arising from the long yellow taproot, giving it the name yellow dock. As the plant matures, flowers appear. These are rather inconspicuous, light green, growing in dense whorls, and only about one-eighth inch wide. Following the flowers are red-brown, papery, three-winged fruits that are produced in late summer and early autumn. The entire plant, upon maturity, can reach up to four feet high.

Parts Used
Roots, young leaves, seeds

Preparation and Uses
Yellow dock is food and medicine. Young leaves have a tart taste and can be harvested and cooked as a potherb. Young roots can be chopped and added to soups or tinctured with alcohol.

Medicinal Benefits and Energetics
Yellow dock is a bitter herb that is cooling and drying and is often used as a detox herb. It is an alterative, laxative, hepatic, cholagogue, and tonic and promotes the flow of bile (Hoffman, 2003). Fresh leaves can be used as a poultice for skin conditions, especially nettle stings. According to folklore, nettle puts the sting in, dock takes the sting out.

Chemical Constituents
The root contains tannins, oxalates, and anthraquinone glycosides that act as a laxative (Winston, 2016).

Growing Yellow Dock
Yellow dock grows naturally in a variety of habitats and can be easily introduced into your yard or garden by scattering the seeds in the fall when they have matured. It establishes itself quite readily.

Safety Precautions
Yellow dock root has laxative effects. Too much can cause diarrhea.

References
Hoffman, D. (2003). *Medical herbalism: The science and practice of herbal medicine.* Rochester, VT: Healing Arts Press.

Winston, D. (2016). "The worst weeds are your best medicine: The common and weedy plant material medica." Lecture notes from 2016 Medicines from the Earth.

YUCCA
(Yucca filamentosa, Y. aloifolia)
Agave Family (Agavaceae)

Description

The agave family is comprised of forty to fifty species of perennials, shrubs, and trees. The yucca that is most familiar on the east coast is *Yucca filamentosa*. It is native to the southeast from southern Virginia to Florida and as far west as

Texas. It has also been planted as an ornamental with cultivated varieties that have escaped and become naturalized. *Yucca aloifolia* is less common and can be distinguished from *Y. filamentosa* by its erect trunk reaching up to twenty-five feet tall. It also has a spike of large white flowers that are tinged with purple. Yucca definitely gets one's attention with its sharp-pointed sword-like leaves. Between June and September, large, white, bell-shaped flowers develop at the top of a tall flowering stalk growing out of the center of a rosette of daggers. Curly, fibrous threads line the edges of long leaves. Its flowers require cross-pollination for a greenish, oblong fruit to develop, and the only pollinator is the yucca moth, which can sometimes be found inside the flowers.

Uses

Yucca is food and medicine. As a food, look for the flower stalk as it starts to emerge from its rosette of leaves. The young stalk is edible. Some are sweeter than others. Peel the stalk first. It has a crunchy texture and is good as a nibble or added to salads. Yucca flowers are also edible and can be added raw to salads, soups, or stir-fries.

Joint Relief

A blend of tinctures to help provide relief for aching joints and arthritis.

- 35 milliliters yucca root
- 30 milliliters black willow
- 25 milliliters meadowsweet
- 15 milliliters Solomon's seal root
- 15 milliliters prickly ash

Combine herbs and add to a 1-ounce tincture bottle. Take one dropper for relief from arthritis and joint pain.

Constituents

Leaves and roots of yucca contain saponins and can be used for soap by gently pounding the leaf or root and rinsing it in water. Saponins are a group of glycosides that have anti-inflammatory properties and are used for arthritis and joint pain.

Safety Precautions

The leaves have sharp, dagger-like tips that can puncture the skin. Yucca should not be confused with yuca (*Manihot esculenta*) that is imported from the tropics and has an edible root that is sold in grocery stores. Sometimes it is even spelled the same.

NUTRITIONAL GLOSSARY

Following is a list of plant properties:

Allyl Sulfides
A cancer preventive found in garlic and onions.

Anthocyanins
May contribute to the prevention of cancer, diabetes, and cardiovascular and neurological diseases (Konczak and Zhang, 2004). Includes mulberries, blueberries, blackberries, elderberries, and grapes.

Antioxidants
A group of vitamins, minerals, and enzymes that neutralize free radicals and are believed to help slow down the aging process. Leafy vegetables including purslane, self-heal, and shepherd's purse as well as nuts and berries are all sources of antioxidants.

B Vitamins
A group of eight essential nutrients that help convert food into energy, create new blood cells, and maintain healthy skin cells, brain cells, and other body tissues. Together they are called the vitamin B complex. The B complex vitamins work together in the body, but they also carry out their own functions (Berry, 2019). Many wild edible foods contain B-complex vitamins, including lambsquarter, nettle, purslane, and red clover (The Herbal Academy, 2021). Legumes, seeds, and nuts also contain B vitamins.

Beta-Carotene
An antioxidant that belongs to the group of carotenoids and is converted to vitamin A in the body. It performs many roles, including an immune booster. Violet, purslane, nettles, dandelion leaf and root, plantain, and wild garlic are just some of the wild plants with beta-carotene, a precursor to vitamin A. All green plants contain pigments known as carotenes. "Beta" carotene makes up the majority of carotene in plants. Carotene and chlorophyll work synergistically to produce vitamins E and K that help convert carotene into vitamin A (Pitchford, 2002). Vitamin A provides protection to surface tissues, from the skin to the mucosal lining of the mouth, nose, throat, and lungs. It helps to build and repair bones and to maintain good vision as well as activate the immune system (Pitchford, 2002).

Bioflavonoids
Useful as antioxidants, antivirals, and anti-inflammatories. They are found in most wild fruits and vegetables.

Boron
A mineral that helps the body to absorb calcium. Sources include wild strawberries, corn salad, dandelion, and nettles.

Calcium
Important for maintaining healthy bones and teeth as well as supporting immune health. For calcium to be absorbed it must be consumed with other nutrients including phosphorus, magnesium, boron, zinc, vitamin D, and vitamin A. Dandelions are one of the best sources of calcium among the wild greens. Other calcium sources include amaranth, lamb's quarters, nettles, watercress, red clover, and purslane (Duke, 1997).

Carvacrol
A compound that helps prevent the breakdown of acetylcholine in the brain and could be a possible alternative for treating Alzheimer's disease. Horsemint is a source of carvacrol.

Coumarins
Natural blood thinners that prevent blood clots and protect against heart disease. Sweet clover and citrus fruits are a good source of coumarins. Avoid these herbs if you take blood-thinning medication.

Ellagic Acid
Antioxidant found in muscadine grapes that may possibly be a cancer preventative.

GLA (Gamma-Linolenic Acid)
A compound that lowers both cholesterol and blood pressure. Oil from evening primrose seeds is a major source of GLA in the plant world.

Genistein

An isoflavone that regulates the immune system and possibly prevents the spread of breast cancer. Sources include red clover and groundnuts.

Indoles

Compounds found in cruciferous vegetables that help prevent cancer.

Iron

Essential for the creation of hemoglobin, which carries oxygen to red blood cells, as well as amino acids, hormones, neurotransmitters, and collagen. A lack of iron can lead to symptoms of anemia, including fatigue, dizziness, brain fog, and chest pain. Vitamin C and B vitamins are necessary for the body to absorb iron. Nettles and dandelion are among the best sources of iron in the plant world. Other sources include legumes, nuts, seeds, and grains.

Isothiocyanates

Cancer preventive found in members of the mustard family.

Lecithin

Emulsifies fat, lowers cholesterol, and protects the cardiovascular system. Helps to maintain brain function by elevating the brain's acetylcholine. Dandelion flowers are an excellent source of lecithin.

Magnesium

A mineral that is vital to enzyme activity and assists in calcium and potassium update. Thistles, purslane, burdock, chickweed, and nuts contain magnesium. Purslane and red clover have particularly high levels of magnesium.

Manganese

Essential nutrient for the formation of digestive enzymes. It promotes the secretion of insulin and helps lower blood sugar levels. Manganese can be found in seeds and whole grains as well as beans, nuts, and leafy greens (Seladi-Schulman, 2018).

Omega-3 Fatty Acids

A type of polyunsaturated fatty acid that protects against heart disease by lowering cholesterol levels and thinning the blood. All dark green leafy vegetables contain omega-3 fatty acids, essential fatty acids that are necessary for good health. They lower blood pressure, reduce cholesterol, lower lipid levels, and reduce clotting. Purslane is one of the best sources of omega-3 fatty acids in the plant world.

Pectins

Pectins reduce cholesterol and protect against diabetes. Many of the wild fruits used to make jelly are high in pectin, including grapes, blackberries, cranberries, rose hips, and plums.

Phosphorus

Essential for growth and maintenance of all body tissues and for healthy bones and teeth. Bittercress, burdock, dandelion, and lamb's quarters all contain phosphorus.

Phytochemicals

Compounds found in plant foods that may help to prevent ailments.

Potassium

Necessary for regulating muscle contractions, including the heartbeat, and maintaining proper fluid balance within the body. It is also an important factor in nerve transmission (Healthwise Staff, 2020). Sources for potassium include purslane, lamb's quarters, dandelion roots, amaranth, corn salad, cranberry, yellow dock, and skullcap.

Protein

Complex compounds that regulate body processes. Nuts, groundnuts, yellow dock, plantain, and wild rice are wild sources of protein.

Pycnogenol

An antioxidant that helps to relieve arthritis symptoms and improve heart health (WebMD, 2021). Grape seeds and pine bark are sources of pycnogenol.

Psyllium

A fiber supplement. Plantain seeds contain psyllium.

Resveratrol

An anti-inflammatory compound produced by certain plants that helps protect them from pests or diseases. Reported to lower cholesterol and the risk of heart disease and is thought to be a cancer-fighting substance. Found in grape leaves, skin, and seeds.

Rutin

A plant pigment that strengthens capillary blood vessels and prevents capillary fragility. Violets and wild pansy flowers and leaves contain rutin.

Serotonin

A neurotransmitter in nerve tissue that is considered essential for relaxation, sleep, and concentration. Black walnuts, hickory nuts, and pecans are the best sources of serotonin in the US.

Sodium

Necessary for maintaining water balance, nerve transmission, and muscle contraction (Healthwise Staff, 2020). Saltmarsh plants contain sodium. Saltwort stores salt in its succulent stem and tastes like pure salt. Bacopa and orache also have a salty taste. Saltmarsh cordgrass (*Spartina* spp.) excretes salt to the surface of the leaves and can be collected by rubbing the leaf blade between your fingers. Other herbs that contain sodium include violets, chickweed, cleavers, bacopa, self-heal, and nettles.

Thymol

Antiseptic compound. The genus *Monarda*, including horsemint and mountain mint, contain thymol.

Tryptophan

An amino acid that is necessary for the production of niacin and used by the brain to produce serotonin. Sources of tryptophan include evening primrose seeds, mustard greens, corn salad, amaranth, and purslane.

Vitamin C

Antioxidant that is necessary for tissue growth and repair. It is also important for the immune system and aids in iron absorption (Healthwise, 2021). It protects the body from oxidative stress and helps to reduce damage from inflammation. Vitamin C is found in fruits and vegetables including pokeweed, lamb's quarters, citrus fruits, pine needles, prickly ash, sumac, rose hips, and purslane.

Vitamin E

An antioxidant that is necessary for normal body functions and found in many foods, including nuts.

Zinc

Helps to make protein and genetic material, and thus is required for fetal development and growth. It also supports the immune system and helps with the body's wound-healing abilities (Healthwise Staff, 2020). Chickweed and hairy bittercress both contain notable levels of zinc (The Herbal Academy, 2021).

References

Berry, J. (2019). "A complete guide to B vitamins." *Medical News Today*. Retrieved from https://www.medicalnewstoday.com/articles/325292.

Duke, J. A. (1997). *The green pharmacy*. Emmaus, PA: Rodale Press.

Healthwise Staff. (2020). "Minerals: Their functions and sources." Retrieved from https://www.uofmhealth.org/health-library/ta3912.

Healthwise Staff, 2020. (2020). "Potassium." Healthwise. Retrieved from https://myhealth.alberta.ca/health/AfterCareInformation/pages/conditions.aspx?hwid=stp1886.

Healthwise Staff. (2021). "Vitamins: Their functions and sources." Retrieved from https://myhealth.alberta.ca/health/Pages/conditions.aspx?hwid=ta3868.

Konczak & Zhang. (2004). "Anthocyanins – more than nature's colors." *J Biomed Biotechnol*. Retrieved from https://pubmed.ncbi.nlm.nih.gov/15577183/.

Pitchford, P. (2002). *Healing with whole foods*. Berkeley, CA: North Atlantic Books.

Seladi-Schulman, J. (2018). "Manganese Deficiency." *Healthline*. Retrieved from https://www.healthline.com/health/manganese-deficiency.

Staughton, J. (2020). *13 Proven benefits of selenium*. Retrieved from https://www.organicfacts.net/selenium.html.

The Herbal Academy. (2021). *A foraged feast: nutritional value of edible wild food*. Retrieved from: https://theherbalacademy.com/wp-content/uploads/2021/06/A-FORAGED-FEAST-NUTRITIONAL-VALUE-OF-EDIBLE-WILD-FOOD-by-Herbal-Academy.pdf

WebMD. (2021). "Health benefits of pycnogenol." Retrieved from https://www.webmd.com/diet/health-benefits-pycnogenol#1.

LIST OF RECIPES

Acorn Cookies	113	Muscadine Shrub	147
B-Happy	40	Nettle Pesto	111
Basic Salve	70	Nut-Berry Cookies	49
Beebalm Oxymel	62	Pain Relief	81
Berry Bites	47	Pawpaw Smoothie	116
Black Cherry Bark Syrup	39	Persimmon Scones	118
Black Cherry Cordial	66	Pine Needle Cough Syrup	38
Black Cherry Juice	47	Poke Sallet	123
Black Cherry Syrup	62	Pollen Cakes	22
Black Gum Wraps	78	Purslane Pickles	125
Black Haw Biscuits	79	Purslane-Tomato Salad	29
Black Haw Puree	79	Respirade	39
Blackberry Brandy	82	Rid-Itch Salve	30
Blackberry Shrub	62	Rose Hip Tea	39
Blueberry Fizz	84	Rose Hip Tincture	39
Blueberry Walnut Scones	80	Rose Petal Honey	25
Brain Booster	74	Rose Water Spritzer	152
Cattail and Thistle Salad	87	Rosemary-Mint Body Butter	30
Chickweed Vinegar	88	Salves	70
Cocoa Cherry Puffs	144	Sassafras Tea	128
Cold-Care	40	Self-Heal Tea	130
Cough Ease	40	Simple Syrup	58
Dandelion-Coconut Macaroons	92	Sleep-Ade, Tea Blend	115
Dandelion Bitters	58	Sleep-eze Tea Blend	57
Dandelion Flower Elixir	67	Sneeze Arrest	35
Detox Soup	23	Soothing Salve	135
Digest-Ade	58	Spicebush Twig Tea	134
Dried Detox Soup Blend	34	Spring Burst Seasoning	120
Elderflower Syrup	94	SSS Tonic	25
Evening Primrose Root Vinegar	96	Stomach Relief	59
Fever-Redux	59	Stone Break Tea	58
Filé Powder	128	Stress Relief	58
Flower-Infused Water	25	Sumac-Ade	28
Green Smoothie with Cleavers	89	Summer Cooler	29
Ground Cherry Vinaigrette	99	Summer Flower Tea	29
Groundnut Soup	100	Thistle Tincture	138
Heart Healthy Tea	59	Wax Myrtle Tea	142
Heartwarming Elixir	67	Wild Bean Salad	48
Herbal Electrolyte Drink	28	Wild Berry Syrup (with sugar)	29
Herbal Insect Repellent	31	Wild Berry Syrup (with honey)	29
Herbal Lotion	70	Wild Blueberry Cordial	66
Herbal Mouthwash	103	Wild Grape Jelly	47
Herbal Smoking Mix	109	Wild Herb Seasoning	46
Hi-C Drink	40	Wild Herb Spread	46
Hot Cider	38	Wild Strawberry Shrub	62
Hot Mulled Apple Cider with Rose Hips and Cranberries	38	Wild Salad Mix	90
Immuni-Tea	34	Wild Vegetable Stir-Fry with Mallow Fruits	106
Joint Relief	156	Wildflower Salad	24
Linden Flower Syrup	62	Yaupon with Turmeric and Cocoa Powder	154
Linden Tea	105	Zest!	124
Mulberry Preserves	108		
Muscadine Preserves	147		

INDEX

Achene, 17
Achillea millefolium. See Yarrow
Acorns, 17, 35, 113
Adaptogens, 22, 28, 40, 57
Allergens, 22, 34
Allergies, 15, 22, 34–35, 40, 98, 111, 120–121, 137, 152
Allium vineale. See Field Garlic
Alterative, 22–23, 86, 123, 126, 141
Amelanchier spp. *See* Serviceberry
Annuals, 9, 88–90, 125, 143, 149–150
Anthocyanocides, 46
Anti-histamines, 34
Antimicrobial, 53, 97, 121, 135
Antioxidants, 28, 53–54, 74, 82, 108, 147, 154
Aperitif, 58, 92
Apios americana. See Groundnuts
Apothecary Method, 66
Arctium minus, A. lappa. See Burdock
Aromatic Oils, 70
Asimina triloba. See Pawpaw
Astringent, 53
Autumn, 34–35
Azalea (*Rhododendron* spp.), 24

Bacopa, 53, 74
Bacopa monnieri. See Bacopa
Bark, 35
Bark, Twigs, and Buds, 15
Basswood, 105
Beautyberry (*Callicarpa americana*), 30–31, 75
Beebalm, 29, 34, 40, 62, 76
Beetle Larvae Oaks, 113
Benefits of Foraging, 12
Berries, 16
Berries, Summer, 28
Berries, Winter, 38
Biennials, 9, 23, 48, 86, 96, 103, 109, 126, 138, 148, 150
Bile, 22–23, 53, 92, 155
Bitter, 53
Bittercress (*Cardamine hirsuta, C. pensylvanica*), 46, 90, 149
Black Gum, 16, 47, 53, 77–78
Black Haw, 79
Black Walnut, 17, 35, 40, 49, 80
Black Willow, 81, 156
Blackberries, 28–29, 47, 62, 82–83
Blood pressure, 4, 59, 90

Blueberries (*Vaccinium* spp.), 16, 28–29, 39, 47, 49, 58, 66, 80, 84
Blueberry, highbush, 84
Blueberry, lowbush, 84
Botany Basics, 14–17
Brahmi, 74
Bulbs, 15, 97
Burdock (*Arctium* spp.), 15, 23, 34, 48, 86
Burdock, Common and Great, 86
Buttercups (*Ranunculus* spp.), 14, 24

Callicarpa americana. See Beautyberry
Camellia sinensis, 56
Capsules, 17
Caretakers, 8
Carminative Herbs, 58
Carrier Oils, 70
Carrot Family, 14
Cashew Family, 30, 136
Cattails, 15, 22, 49, 87
Cercis canadensis. See Redbud
Chickweed, 30, 53, 88
Chlorophyll, 4, 46, 104, 139
Cholagogues, 22
Choloretics, 22
Circulatory system, 59
Cirsium spp., *See* Thistle
Cleavers (*Galium aparine*), 22–23, 53, 89
Cold and Flu Season, 39
Common Ailments, 46, 52, 57
Congestion, 22, 24, 34, 39, 98, 142, 150
Cooling Herbs, 28, 53, 54, 130, 132
Cordials, 39, 66
Corms, 15
Corn Salad (*Valerianella* spp.), 38, 46, 90
Corticoids, 22
Corylus americana. See Hazelnut
Crabapple, Narrow-leaf, 91
Cranberries (*Vaccinium macrocarpon*), 58
Cross-pollinated, 16, 101, 116, 156
Cultivating Weeds, 8–9
Curly Dock. *See* Yellow Dock

Dandelion, 15, 22–24, 34, 53, 58, 67, 90, 92–93
Dandelion root, 34, 58
Decoctions, 56
Dehiscent fruits, 16
Demulcent herbs, 54, 88, 107, 109, 141

Detoxification, 22–23, 48, 92, 111
Dewberries, 82–83
Diaphoretics, 22, 28, 76, 86, 94, 97–98, 104–105, 128, 153
Dicots, 14
Digestif, 58
Digestion, 23, 52, 58, 66, 92, 150, 153
Digestive bitters, 58
Diospyrus virginiana. See Persimmon
Diuretics, 22–23, 52, 58, 84, 86, 89, 92, 98, 105, 111, 123, 130, 136, 152–153
"Doctrine of Signatures", 80
Drupes, 16
Dry Fruits, 16–17
Drying Herbs, 54
Duke, Dr. James, 4

Edible Flowers, 24–25
Elder (*Sambucus canadensis*), 94–95
Elderflower, 28, 34, 39, 59, 94
Electrolytes, 28
Elixirs, 67
Energetics, 53–54
Essential oils, 4, 30–31, 53, 56, 70, 98, 103, 152–153
Evening Primrose (*Oenothera biennis*), 15, 17, 23, 29, 34, 48, 96
Evening Primrose Seeds, 34, 40, 96
Expectorants, 34, 39, 88, 109, 121, 144

Fall Cleansing, 34
Field Garlic, 34, 46, 97, 100, 125
Filberts, 101
Five Tastes, Chinese Medicine, 52
Fixed oils, 29–30, 70, 88, 121
Flavonoids, 28, 53–54, 57, 81–82, 84, 88, 92, 94, 97–98, 105, 107, 109, 120–121, 132, 142, 148, 153–154
Fleshy Fruits, 16
Flower Arrangements, 16
Flower Types
Indistinguishable, 16
    Irregular, 16
    Regular, 16
    Flower-Infused Water, 25
Flowers, 9, 16, 24
Flowers, Male and Female, 16, 77, 87, 111, 128, 154
Folk Method, 66
Follicle, 16, 124
Food Farmacy, 43
Forager's Garden, 8–9
Foraging Ethics, 8
Foraging Habitats, 8
Forest Bathing, 4
Forest Bathing, Practicing, 4–5

Fruit Syrups, 47
Fruits, 16–17

Galium aparine. See Cleavers
Garlic Mustard (*Alliaria petiolata*), 46, 90, 149
Gaylussacia spp., 84
Ghost Pipe. *See* Indian Pipe
Glycerin, 56, 66
Glycerites, 66
Goldenrod, 24, 34–35, 40, 98
Goldenrod, Sweet, 34, 98
Grapes, Muscadine (*Vitis rotundifolia*), 146–147
Green Cuisine, 46
Greens, Backyard, 46
Greens, Spring, 23
Greens, Summer, 29, 125
Greens, Winter, 38
Ground Cherry, 99
Groundnuts, 15, 34, 49, 100

Harvesting Flowers, 24–25
Hawthorn (*Crataegus* spp.), 16, 38, 40, 47, 53, 59, 67
Hazelnut, 17, 35, 49, 101
Heal-all. *See* Self-Heal
Heart Health, 59, 119
Heat and Hydration, 28
Heating Herbs, 53–54
Hemlock, Poison (*Conium maculatum*), 14
Hemlock, Water (*Cicuta maculata*), 14, 95
Herb Oil, Dried, 70
Herb Oil, Fresh, 70
Herb Teas, Cooling, 28
Herbal Syrups, 62
Herbal Vinegars, 62
Herbs with Salt, 53
Hibiscus moscheutos. See Rose Mallow
Hibiscus spp., *See* Mallow
Hi-C Drink, 40
Hickory, 17, 35, 49, 102, 139
Histamine, 34, 111
Homeostasis, 4
Honeysuckle (*Lonicera japonica*), 14, 24–25, 90
Horsemint, 39, 103
Huckleberries, 16, 84
Hydrochloric acid, 52
Hypericum punctatum. See St. John's wort

Ilex vomitoria. See Yaupon
Immune System, 34, 38–40, 46, 119, 130, 139, 152
Indehiscent Dry Fruits, 17
Indian Pipe, 81, 104
Infusions, Cold, 56
Infusions, Hot, 56

Infusions, Solar, 56
Inner Bark, 25, 39, 41, 81, 124, 144
Insect Bites and Stings, 30
Insect Repellent, 30–31, 75, 120, 142
Invasive Aliens, 46, 153

Jewelweed (*Impatiens capensis*), 30
Journal, Log, 5
Journaling, 5–6
Juglans nigra. See Black Walnut
Juices, 47

Kidney and Bladder Health, 58
Kitchen Lab, 46–49

Lactuca canadensis. See Wild Lettuce
Laportea canadensis. See Nettle, Wood
Laxatives, 22–23, 58, 92, 108, 121, 152, 155
Leaves, 15–16
Lectins, 48, 52, 143
Legumes, 16, 47–48, 100
Lichen, Fruticose, 139
Lifestyle, Foraging, 1
Limonene, 54
Linden (*Tilia americana*), 29, 40, 57–59, 62, 105, 115
Lindera benzoin. See Spicebush
Liquid pectin, 47, 91
Liver Cleansers, 23, 138
Lotions, 70
Lycopus virginica, L. americana. See Bugleweed
Lymphatic Cleanser, 23, 126

Mache, 90
Mallow (*Hibiscus* spp.), 29, 34, 39, 54, 58, 106–107
Mallow Family, 105–107
Mallow, Common, 106
Malva neglecta. See Mallow, Common
Marc, 56
Menstruum, 56, 70
Metabolites, 4
Metabolites, Primary, 4
Metabolites, Secondary, 4
Microgreens, 46
Mind-body Interaction, 4
Mindfulness, 5, 14
Mints, 75–76, 85, 103, 130, 132
Moistening Herbs, 39, 54
Monarda didyma. See Beebalm
Monarda punctata. See Horsemint
Monocots, 14
Monotropa uniflora. See Indian Pipe
Mood Elevators, 40, 96
Moonseed (*Menispermum canadense*), 147
Morella cerifera. See Wax Myrtle

Morus alba. See Mulberry, White
Morus rubra. See Mulberry, Red
Mucilage, 53–54, 56, 66, 99, 105–107, 109, 121, 150
Mulberries, 28–29, 108
Mulberry, Red, 108
Mulberry, White, 108
Mullein, 34–35, 40, 109–110
Multi-vitamins, 38
Mushrooms, 15, 104
Mustard Family, 4, 23–24, 46, 53, 149–150

N. biflora. See Swamp Black Gum
Nervine Sedatives, 57
Nervine Stimulants, 57, 76
Nervine Tonics, 57, 74, 132
Nervines, 57, 79, 135, 144, 148, 152
Nettle Seed, 111
Nettle, Wood, 111
Nettles (*Urtica dioica*), 23, 30, 34–35, 46, 58, 111–112
Nut Milk, 47, 102
Nuts
Acorns (*Quercus* spp.), 17, 35, 113
    Beechnuts (*Fagus grandifolia*), 17, 35, 49
    Black Walnut (*Juglans nigra*), 17, 35, 40, 49, 80
    Hazelnuts (*Corylus americana, C. cornuta*), 17, 35, 49, 101
    Nyssa aquatica. See Water Tupelo
Nyssa sylvatica. See Black Gum

Oaks, 113–114
Oenothera biennis. See Evening Primrose
Ogeechee gum (*Nyssa ogeche*), 77
Oil Infusions, 25, 70, 109, 142
Organoleptics, 5
Oxalis spp. *See* Sorrel, Wood
Oxymels, 62

P. lanceolata. See Plantain
Passiflora incarnata. See Passionvine
Passionvine (*Passiflora incarnata*), 24, 29, 57–59, 109, 115
Pawpaw, 15–16, 47, 116–117
Pecan (*Carya illinoensis*), 102, 111
Pectin, 47, 56, 77, 82, 84, 91, 122, 146
People-Plant Relationships, 4
Peppergrass (*Lepidium virginicum*), 90, 149
Peppervine (*Ampelopsis arborea*), 147
Perennials, 9, 38, 74, 85, 92, 103–104, 106, 111, 121, 123, 132, 135, 141, 150, 153, 155–156
Persimmon, 16, 47, 53, 118
Photosynthesis, 15, 46, 139
Physalis spp. *See* Ground Cherry
Phytochemicals, 4, 46, 52, 56
Phytolacca americana. See Poke

Phytoncides, 4
Pine Needle Tea, 38, 119
Pine Resin, 119–120
Pinus spp. *See* Pine
Plant Cycles, 19
Plant Families, 17
Plant Features, 15–17
Plant Poisoning, 14
Plant Sketching, 6
Plantago major. See Plantain
Plantain (*Plantago* spp.), 30, 34, 39–40, 58–59, 121
Plantain, Common, 121
Plantain, Lance-Leaved, 121
Plum, 16, 53, 122
Plum, American (*P. americana*), 122
Plum, Beach (*P. maritima*), 122
Plum, Chickasaw (*P. angustifolia*), 122
Poison Ivy (*Toxicodendron radicans*), 5, 14, 30–31, 113, 120–121
Poison Oak, 30
Poison Sumac, 30, 136–137
Poisonous Flowers, 24
Poisonous Legumes, 48
Poisonous Plants, 14, 17
Poke, 23, 123
Pokeberries (*Phytolacca americana*), 14
Pollen
Cattails, 22, 87
    Pines, 22, 46, 119–120
    Pome, 16
Portulaca oleracea. See Purslane
Predicting Winter, 118
Prickly ash (*Zanthoxylum clava-herculis*), 35, 124
Prickly ash (*Zanthoxylum* spp.), 16, 57, 59, 74
Proteinase Inhibitors, 52
Prunella vulgaris. See Self-Heal
Prunus serotina. See Wild Black Cherry
Prunus spp. *See* Plum
Pungent, 53–54
Purslane, 29, 125

Quercus spp. *See* Oaks

Raspberries, 28, 82–83, 138
Redbud (*Cercis canadensis*), 24, 48, 127
Respiratory Health, 39
Rhizomes, 15, 87, 94, 112, 117, 128, 132, 150
Rhus spp. *See* Sumac
Roots, 15
Roots, Adventitious, 15
Roots, Primary, 15, 128
Rosa spp. *See* Wild Rose
Rose Family, 53–54, 82, 91, 122, 131, 144
Rose Mallow, 106
Rose Petal Honey, 25, 152

Rubus spp., 82
Rumex acetosella. See Sorrel, Sheep
Rumex crispus. See Yellow Dock

Salix nigra. See Black Willow
Salt, 52
Salt Marsh Plants, 52–53
Saltmarsh Cordgrass (*Spartina* spp.), 53
Saltwort (*Salicornia* spp.), 53
Salves, 30, 70, 135
Samara, 17
Sambucus nigra. See Elder
Sassafras, 15, 24–25, 54, 128–129
Sassafras albidum. See Sassafras
Sassafras Flowers, 24
Saving Seeds, 35
Scutellaria lateriflora. See Skullcap
Sea-beach orach (*Atriplex* spp.), 53
Seasonal Affective Disorder (SAD), 40
Seasonings and Spices, 52–54
Seed Dispersal, 16
Seeds, 9, 15–17
Self-Heal, 130
Self-pollination, 16
Serotonin, 40, 80, 96, 111
Serviceberry, 131
Shagbark hickory (*Carya ovata*), 102
Shellbark hickory (*C. laciniosa*), 102
Shepherd's Purse (*Capsella bursa-pastoris*), 149–150
Shinrin-Yoku, 4
Shrubs, 62
Six Tastes, Ayurveda, 52–53
Skin Protection, 29–30
Skullcap (*Scutellaria lateriflora*), 57–59, 115, 132
Slippery Elm, 54
Solidago spp. *See* Goldenrod
Solubility, 56, 66
Solvents, 56
Sorrel, 133
Sorrel, Sheep, 38, 53, 133
Sorrel, Wood, 14, 24, 53, 133
Soups, 48
Sour, 53
Sowing Seeds, 9
Spicebush, 25, 38, 134
Spotted spurge (*Euphorbia* spp.), 125
Spring, 22–25
Spring Scents, 24
Spring Tonics, 22, 25, 89
St. John's wort (*Hypericum punctatum*), 40, 57–59, 135
Stellaria media. See Chickweed
Stems, 15
Stinging Nettle (*Urtica dioica*), 23, 30, 58, 111

Stolons, 15
Stonebreak (*Phyllanthus niruri*), 58
Stress, 57
Stress Management, 39
Strophostyles helvola, S. umbellata. See Wild Beans
Strychnine, 24
Succession, 9, 83
Sumac (*Rhus* spp.), 28–29, 39, 47, 53, 136–137
Sumac, Poison (*Toxicodendron vernix*), 30, 136
Sumac, Smooth (*Rhus glabra*), 136
Sumac, Staghorn (*Rhus typhina*), 136
Sumac, Winged (*Rhus copallinum*), 136
Summer, 28–31
Sustainable Foraging, 8–9
Sustainable Harvesting, 8
Swamp Black Gum, 77
Sweet, 53
Sweet Birch, 25, 81
Synergy, 57
Syrups, 29, 38–39, 47, 58, 62

Tannin, 53–54, 56, 66, 81–82, 84, 89, 91, 99, 105, 109,
    113–114, 121, 124, 128, 136, 142, 144, 153, 155
Taproots, 15, 23, 92, 96, 117, 120, 138, 155
Taraxacum officinale. See Dandelion
Taste Buds, 15, 52
Taste Test, 15, 52
Tastes, 5, 52–53, 78, 87
Tasting Herbs, 52
Tea Blending, 56–57, 59
Tea Formulation, 56–57
Teas, Herbal, 28, 56–59
Teas, Winter, 38
Thistle (*Silybum marianum, Cirsium* spp.), 23, 138
Thistles, 22, 48, 87, 93
Thymol, 76, 103
Tilia americana. See Linden
Tinctures, 39, 66, 138
Tisanes, 56
Tonics
Sassafras, 25
    Spicebush, 25
    Sweet birch, 25
    Toothwort (*Cardamine* spp.), 150
Tree Sap, 25
Tree Talk, 41
Trifolium pratense. See Red Clover
Tryptophan, 40, 96
Tubers, 15, 100
Typha latifolia, T. angustifolia. See Cattails

Umami   , 52
Urtica dioica. See Nettles, Stinging
Usnea, 40, 66, 139–140

Vaccinium spp., 39, 58, 84
Valerianella radiata, V. locusta. See Corn Salad
Vascular plants, 14
Verbascum thapsus. See Mullein
Viburnum prunifolium. See Black Haw
Viola spp. *See* Violet
Violet, 24–25, 30, 39–40, 53, 141
Violet, Halberd-leaf violet (*V. hastata*), 141
Virginia Creeper (*Parthenocissus quinquefolia*),
    14, 147
Vitamin C, 38–40, 82, 88, 91, 94, 97, 99, 107, 116,
    119, 127, 141, 152
Vitis spp. *See* Wild Grapes
Volatile oils, 56, 70, 105, 128–129, 132
Voucher Specimens, 5–6

Water Hemlock (*Cicuta maculata*), 14, 95
Water Hyssop. *See Bacopa*
Water Tupelo, 77
Watercress (*Nasturtium officinale*), 150
Wax myrtle (*Morella cerifera*), 30, 57, 59, 142
Wetlands, 48–49, 74, 77, 85, 87
Wild Beans, 4
Wild Beans (*Strophostyles* spp. and *Phaseolus
    polystachios*), 48, 143
Wild Black Cherry, 34, 144
Wild Cherry (*Prunus serotina*), 35, 53–54, 138,
    144–145
Wild Food Habitat, 8
Wild Garden, 8–9
Wild Garden, Maintenance, 9
Wild Grapes, 47, 146–147
Wild Jellies, Jams, and Juices, 47
Wild Lettuce, 57, 81, 93, 109, 115, 148
Wild Mustards, 4, 23–24, 34, 38, 46, 90, 149
Wild Rose, 24, 84, 152
Wild versus Tame, 4
Winston, David, 52, 111
Winter, 38–41
Winter cress; Yellow Rocket (*Barbarea vulgaris, B.
    verna*), 150
Wood sorrel (*Oxalis* spp.), 14, 24, 53, 133

Yarrow, 28, 30, 59, 153
Yaupon, 109, 120, 154
Yellow Dock (*Rumex crispus*), 15, 23, 30, 34, 48,
    53, 58, 155
Yellow Jessamine (*Gelsemium sempervirens*), 14, 24
Yucca, 156
Yucca filamentosa, Y. aloifolia. See Yucca

Z. clava-herculis. See Prickly Ash
Zanthoxylum americanum. See Prickly Ash

ACKNOWLEDGMENTS

First and foremost, I want to acknowledge Dr. James Duke who changed my life completely when he introduced me to the world of medicinal plants. Since then, the teachers have been many: presenters at herbal gatherings who willingly shared their information and knowledge, my teachers at Tai Sophia (now Maryland University of Integrative Health), personal mentors (too many to name) who added to my knowledge base, and, most of all, nature herself.

ABOUT THE AUTHOR

Vickie Shufer is a forager, naturalist, and an herbalist. Growing up on a farm in rural Kentucky, gathering wild berries in the summer and nuts in the fall were a part of life. Her passion for the outdoors and wild plants prompted her to get an undergraduate degree in outdoor recreation and a master's degree in therapeutic herbalism. From 1994 to 2014, she was the editor and publisher of "The Wild Foods Forum" newsletter, author of *The Everything Guide to Foraging*, and co-author of several regional river guides. In 2016, the American Botanical Council published her article on yaupon holly in *Herbalgram* magazine.

Vickie is currently the owner of Wild Woods Farm, an eleven-acre certified native nursery where she grows and sells native and medicinal plants and plant products. The farm serves as an outdoor classroom where Vickie teaches others how to identify, harvest, and use wild plants for food and medicine. She demonstrates how to live the life of a forager and guides others to connect with plants for food and medicine. For more information on Vickie and what she offers, visit wildwoodsfarm.us/.